Computing in Musicology

An International Directory of Applications

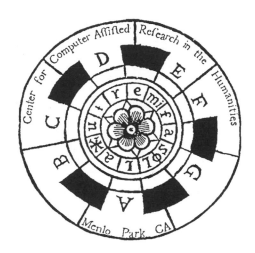

Center for Computer Assisted Research in the Humanities
Menlo Park, CA

Volume 8   1992

© 1992 Center for Computer Assisted Research in the Humanities

ISBN 0-936943-06-6
ISSN 1057-9478

Printed on acid-free recycled paper by George Lithograph, San Francisco, CA

Center for Computer Assisted Research in the Humanities
525 Middlefield Road, Suite 120
Menlo Park, CA 94025-3443
XB.L36@Forsythe.Stanford.Edu
XB.L36@Stanford.Bitnet

Preface

In this issue of *Computing in Musicology* we provide the broadest spectrum yet of computer applications in the scholarly exploration of musical topics. Some applications, such as the lead article by Sandra Pinegar, are concerned with new approaches to old questions, while others, such as Hermann Gottschewski's enquiry into the mathematical proportions of elapsed time in sound recordings, are concerned with new questions. In all, this issue provides 75 contributions from 18 nations. A broad diversity of sub-disciplines—including theory, history, bibliography, cognitive studies, style simulation, data representation, and sound analysis and control—is also included.

The rise of networks as a medium of dissemination seems to mark a paradigm shift in how we work with information that may be more profound than the mere absorption of computers into our midst. This was the first year when our mail began to abound with references to programs and data files, some of them of considerable potential interest to our readers, that could be "ftp-ed". The decoding of this new verb was too cumbersome to put in a footnote, and our enquiry resulted instead in a tutorial. We hasten to disclaim any expertise in this area. We provide background and resource information, together with models of address structures and commands that work for us, and we hope that there is enough common ground to enable novices to further explore the possibilities represented. Readers are encouraged to seek expert advice, when available, in their local computing environments.

While they may pose technical obstacles to novice users, network services can also pose challenges of great magnitude to traditional academic practices. In the forum section, two experienced moderators of online services offer their perspectives on the value of these new models of communication, while general questions of information ownership are framed by Brian Kahin of the Kennedy School of Government.

Our enquiry into the present state of music notation programs continues vigorously, although we felt that after last year's round with Ravel's *Gaspard de la nuit*, our faithful contributors deserved a break, and we have let them off the hook with two contributions each instead of three and set pieces that explore fairly general matters, such as cues within cues and the setting of recitatives. Responses to Don Byrd's quiz (1991) will interest the software community in the notational complexities that they document.

This year more than ever we are indebted to our friends, contributors, colleagues, and staff. The members of our advisory board have provided many valuable suggestions including the idea of producing an article on networks. Among the many people who helped with the network article, Thomas J. Mathiesen and Lee Rothfarb provided much valuable information based on their own experiences. Don Byrd has been very patient in pursuing notational esoterica to check answers to the music notation quiz. The music software contributors continue to provide very timely and tidy responses to our queries. The quality of this year's free contributions concerning applications was unsurpassed. We hasten to extend our cordial thanks to all of these associates and to our industrious staff members Edmund Correia Jr., Meredith Berger, Frances Bennion, Nicholas Carter, and Steven Rasmussen.

September 22, 1992   *Menlo Park, CA*

Contents

Author/Short Title List

Text Applications

Sandra Pinegar:

THEMA

Thema is a textual database presently comprising transcriptions from thirty-seven thirteenth- and early fourteenth-century manuscript copies of Latin treatises dealing with the topic of "measurable music." Begun in the context of research for a doctoral dissertation, *Thema* will soon begin a process of broadening its range of texts both topically and chronologically, and it is hoped that it will become available through an online listserver from a mainframe in an academic environment.

The principal objective in the formation of *Thema* was that each transcription should "mirror" the original text as closely as possible, as in a photographic facsimile. Thus, individual lines of texts have the same length and content as those in the manuscript, and encoding symbols identify foliation and columns, flourished minor initials, paragraph signs, musical examples, and other elements. Texts of the historical period represented by the "core" of this database are highly abbreviated, and one of the distinctive characteristics of *Thema* is a system of numerical tagging that encodes the abbreviations. This allows determination of the density of abbreviations, documentation of changes in scribal characteristics, tracing some scribal errors to misreadings of abbreviated words found in other exemplars, and comparison between two or more copies of a text, between gatherings, text columns, or other sections of one copy, and between two or more independent texts.

Thema materials are transportable as ASCII files for use in a variety of word processing and concordance or "word-crunching" programs and for use with a variety of hardware configurations. It was developed in an MS-DOS environment. The database currently takes up about two megabytes.

The accompanying illustration is taken from a manuscript copy (Vatican Library lat. 5325) of the treatise "De mensurabili musica" attributed to Johannes de Garlandia. Little is known about the life of this thirteenth-century master, who worked in Paris in the second quarter of the century. This treatise was repeatedly copied and its classification of consonant and dissonant intervals greatly influenced later writers.

Treatises in Latin were full of abbreviations, but the style of writing these abbreviations changed over time and place as well as from person to person. By encoding a large body of theoretical material to reflect scribal style, as shown here, one can trace similarities in the presentation of the material. Each abbreviation sign carries

A *THEMA* model.

One folio [12^v] from the treatise "De mensurabili musica" [Vatican Library lat. 5325] attributed to Johannes de Garlandia.

THEMA

< A GAR >

< M VAT >

< F 12v >

!!Habito de ipsa87 plana musica que

immensurabilis46 dicitur91 nec39 est1 presens17 intencio48

de ipsa87 mensurabilis [[d]] que33 organum1 dicitur91

quantum33 ad nos prout19 organum1 generale&

dicitur. ad omnem5 mensurabilem31 musicam1

vnde91 organum1. et2 est species91 tocius mensurabilis31 musice.&

et2 est1 genus91 diuersimode17 tamen91 prout19 dictum48 est1 superius23.

$Sciendum est1 ergo91 quod ipsius87 organi generaliter66

accepti tres6 sunt species91. Discantus. Copula. Organum1&

de quibus21 dicendum91 est1 per23 ordinem. Discantus est1

aliquorum25 cantuum1 sonancia secundum92 modum1 et2 secundum91

equipollentis sui equipollenciam. Sed2 quia92

in1 huius9 discantu consistit maneries17 siue91 modus. et2

de speciebus92 ipsius87 modi siue91 maneriei17. et2 gratia92 huius9 maneriei17&

ac specierum91 eius plura17 alia uidebimus9. Maneries17&

eius appellatur43 quicquid33 mensuratione91 temporis23

uidelicet91 per23 longas uel43 per23 breues concurrit29. Sunt1

ergo91 sex6 species91 ipsius91 maneriei17. quarum25 tres6 dicuntur

mensurabiles74 tres6 uero17 ultra39 mensurabiles74 idest8 ultra39 rectam&

mensuram31 se habentes53. $Iste uero17 dicuntur93 mensurabiles74&

scilicet8 prima17. et2 secunda6. et2 sexta6. $Iste autem

ultra39 mensurabiles74. uidelicet93 tertia6. quarta4. et2 quinta4. prima17. enim8 procedit19&

ex una longa et2 altera17 breui et2 altera17 longa3&

et2 sic usque in infinitum5. Secunda91 fit e conuerso46

uidelicet91 ex una breui et2 alia longa. et2 altera17

breui. Tercia ex una longa et2 duabus6 breuibus21

< F 13r >

Key to selected tags

17 = an apostrophe-like stroke which can stand for *er*, *re*, *ri*, *ir*, or more rarely *ur* or *iter*.

31 = a macron over an *m* or *n* that expands to a vowel plus another *m* or *n*. [A prevalent root is *men [$\bar{m}$] sur-*.]

91 = a "sieve" coding file for abbreviations that do not conform to a pattern.

A THEMA encoding of the folio shown opposite.

a separate numerical code; these codes are suffixed to the full word that results from "realizing" the abbreviation. The density of abbreviations and changes in scribal characteristics can be examined more consistently by machine than by recollection and photographic comparison.

The *THEMA* System for Encoding Scribal Abbreviations

Scribes of the Middle Ages found many ways to shorten their tasks. Like language itself, scribal practice varied over distance and evolved over time, for there were no textbooks, no standards committees, and no oral tradition by which to sanction or publicize any one approach. The scripts for more than 14,000 abbreviations found in Latin documents of the Middle Ages are itemized in Adriano Cappelli's *Dizionario di abbreviature latine ed italiane* (6th edn., Milan: Ulrico Hoepli, 1960). This listing does not begin to exhaust the details of the practice of *abbreviatura*.

Abbreviations could come about in several ways. Many abbreviations have multiple uses and their meaning must be inferred from the context. Some common approaches to the formation of abbreviations follow:

1. They could take the form of one letter to represent a full syllable, *e.g.*

$$\text{P} = \text{P} = pro$$
$$\text{p} = \text{p/} = per, por, \text{ or } par$$
$$\text{qp} = quo$$

2. They could take selected letters to represent a full word, *e.g.*

$$\text{pfc} = \text{p/fc} = perfect$$

3. They could conform to an arbitrary convention, *e.g.*

$$4 = 4 = -rum$$
$$\sim = -ur$$
$$9 = 9 \text{ (for initial syllable)} = co-, con-, \text{ or } com-$$

but please note
9 (for terminal syllable) = *-us*
when following the letters b, t, i, m, e, d, c, p, or l

THEMA representation of special features.

The large painted capital in the illustration on p. 12 is encoded "!!". The flourished minor initials on this later folio from the same treatise are encoded "!".

4. They could take the form of one letter plus (a) a symbol or (b) a second letter and a symbol. These combination abbreviations are the ones that are most common over a vowel. The most common symbol was the horizontal bar resembling a macron used over a vowel. This symbol could take the form of a dot, an apostrophe, or a wavy line (tilde), but the meaning was the same:

a. a bar over a vowel most often stands for an omitted m or n following the vowel, *e.g.*

$$\bar{a} = an$$
$$\bar{\iota} = is \text{ (but also } ivi, \; iver)$$
$$\bar{o} = -io, \; -ion-$$

b. some other letter + symbol conventions cover such pronouns as

$$\text{ꝗ} = q- = qua$$
$$\bar{\text{ꝗ}} = q- = que$$
$$\text{ꝗ} = q'' = qui$$

c. some letter + letter + symbol abbreviations include

$$ƀꝫ = bz = -bus$$
$$ſƀ = sb.\% = sub$$

5. Another large class of abbreviations consists of cases in which a single symbol represents an entire word. This practice is associated with monosyllabic words but may pertain to commonly used polysyllabic words and may be idiosyncratic to one particular source. For example, in the British Museum's holding of the treatise known as *Anonymous 4*, the words *longa* and *longam* occur so often that the scribe eventually indicates them as ".1.".

One of the major difficulties in tagging abbreviations for computerized textual analysis lies in their use in tandem with one another. For example,

$$\text{ꝯuēit} = \text{9uēit} \sim = conuenitur$$

In order to deal with such complexities, the identifiers used for tagging abbreviations must meet many requirements. It is fundamentally clear that they must differ from the text itself so that the program will recognize them as tags. Numerical values serve well for this purpose, but it is essential that as few as possible be used and that as much information as possible should be represented by them. In the system described here, the word itself is always given in full and in two-digit numbers; each digit may have an independent function.

In the sample document shown, the following general scheme pertains. When a single symbol or only macrons are used within a single word, then an odd number is used to indicate position and frequency of appearance. Some examples follow:

1 = a macron representing m or n in the final syllable
3 = a macron is found in another syllable
5 = two macrons are used
7 = three macrons are used

Even numbers as tags indicate that there are two symbols or a symbol in conjunction with one or more macrons in a single word. The specific even number is produced by adding the odd numbers for the separate symbols or combinations of macrons. This means that single even numbers can stand for diverse combinations of abbreviations, *e.g.*

two macrons (5) + i- = 50
as in *ordinationem* presented as *ordiātōnē*

There are ten combinations that can produce the number 40.

The odd/even numbering system identifies about three-quarters of the abbreviations being used in the manuscript studies. In general, lower numbers indicate greater frequency of occurrence and vice-versa.

Words that fall outside the limits of the system are collected in a special file and are indicated with the prefix "9". This file also acts as a filter by collecting data on abbreviations. Not all differences in the use of conventional abbreviations are significant. For example the ō tagged as 45 can mean "io," "ion," or "iom," but the distinction between the three would not seem to yield useful information, given that the proper realization of the word is provided in the machine transcription.

No list of each word/abbreviation combination is retained because concordances that provide this information can easily be generated with the *Oxford Concordance Program*, which has been enormously helpful in pursuing the final goal of studying scribal style. *Sidekick* functions well in the management of the non-conforming abbreviations, albeit by believing them to be telephone numbers.

....

The work of **Sandra Pinegar**, *235 W. 102nd Street, 9V, New York, NY 10025; tel. (212) 222-4270, originates in her doctoral thesis (Columbia University), "Textual and Conceptual Relationships Among Theoretical Writings on Mensurable Music during the Thirteenth and Early Fourteenth Centuries."*

Thomas Mathiesen:
The *Thesaurus Musicarum Latinarum*

The *Thesaurus Musicarum Latinarum* is a collaborative project which aims to make available in machine-readable form all Latin writings on music theory from the Middle Ages and the Renaissance [see *CM 1990,* p. 133, and *1991*, pp. 37-9]. The philosophy behind the *Thesaurus Musicarum Latinarum* is significantly different from that of *THEMA* [preceding article]. Whereas *THEMA* attempts to encode manuscript sources and all their idiosyncracies, the aim of the *TML* is to capture the content of early treatises from available modern editions. We are thus able to show below in addition to the same passage given in the first two illustrations from a Vatican manuscript and the *THEMA* database the same material in the nineteenth-century edition of Coussemaker (*Scriptorum de musica medii aevi nova serie,* Paris, 1864-76) and in a *TML* encoding stored in a listserver.

The *TML* has a special system for encoding musical incipits [given in *CM 1991*, pp. 38f]. In the second set of examples [p. 20], the passage from Coussemaker's edition (the "model") contains musical examples which are identified by subscripted numbers in the encoding. We do not see the actual code, which is stored separately. Further information about the *TML*, which has recently received a grant for the years 1992-94 from the National Endowment for the Humanities, can be found in the article "Using Networks" [pp. 31-60].

Habito de ipsa plana musica que immensurabilis dicitur, nunc est presens intentio de ipsa mensurabili, que organum dicitur, quantum ad nos prout organum generale dicitur ad omnem mensurabilem musicam. Unde organum et est species totius mensurabilis musice, et est genus diversimode tamen, prout dictum est superius. Sciendum ergo quod ipsius organi generaliter accepte tres sunt species : discantus, copula, organum, de quibus dicendum est per ordinem.

Discantus est aliquorum cantuum sonantia secundum modum et secundum equipollentis sui equipollentiam. Sed quia in hujus modi discantu consistit maneries sive modus, et de speciebus ipsius modi vel maneriei, et igitur hujus modi maneriei ac specierum ejus plura videbimus.

Maneries ejus appellatur quidquid mensuratione temporis, videlicet per longas, vel per breves concurrit. Sunt ergo sex species ejus maneriei, quarum tres dicuntur mensurabiles; tres vero ultra mensuram se habentes. Iste vero dicuntur mensurabiles, scilicet prima et secunda et sexta. Iste autem ultra mensurabiles, videlicet tertia, quarta et quinta.

Prima enim procedit ex una longa et alia brevi, et altera longa, et sic usque in infinitum.

Secunda fit e converso, videlicet ex una brevi et alia longa, et altera brevi.

Tertia ex una longa et duabus brevibus, et una longa.

A TML model: the Coussemaker edition of "De mensurabili musica."

```
Data entry: John Snyder
Checked by: Luminita Aluas
Approved by: Thomas J. Mathiesen

Coussemaker Scriptores, vol. I

[-175-] Johannis de Garlandia

De musica mensurabili

Habito de ipsa plana musica que immensurabilis dicitur, nunc est presens
intentio de ipsa mensurabili, que organum dicitur, quantum ad nos prout
organum generale dicitur ad omnem mensurabilem musicam. Unde organum et est
species totius mensurabilis musice, et est genus diversimode tamen, prout
dictum est superius. Sciendum ergo quod ipsius organi generaliter accepte tres
sunt species: discantus, copula, organum, de quibus dicendum est per ordinem.
Discantus est aliquorum cantuum sonantia secundum modum et secundum
equipollentis sui equipollentiam. Sed quia in hujus modi discantu consistit
maneries sive modus, et de speciebus ipsius modi vel maneriei, et igitur hujus
modi maneriei ac specierum ejus plura videbimus.
Maneries ejus appellatur quidquid mensuratione temporis, videlicet per longas,
vel per breves concurrit. Sunt ergo sex species ejus maneriei, quarum tres
dicuntur mensurabiles; tres vero ultra mensuram se habentes. Iste vero
dicuntur mensurabiles, scilicet prima et secunda et sexta. Iste autem ultra
mensurabiles, videlicet tertia, quarta et quinta.
Prima enim procedit ex una longa et alia brevi, et altera longa, et sic usque
in infinitum.
Secunda fit e converso, videlicet ex una brevi et alia longa, et altera brevi.
Tertia ex una longa et duabus brevibus, et una longa.
```

A *TML* encoding.

Prima vero talis est : longa ante longam valet longam et brevem.

Secunda vero talis est : si multitudo brevium fuerit in aliquo loco, semper debemus facere quod equipolleant longis.

Tertia vero talis est : si multitudo brevium fuerit in aliquo loco, quando brevis plus appropinquat fini, tanto debet longior proferri.

Modus perfectus dicitur esse, quandocumque ita est quod aliquis modus desinit per talem quantitatem vel per talem modum, sicuti per illam qua incipit. Dicitur modus perfectus, ut dicatur prima longa, altera brevis, et altera longa; et sic de singulis modis vel manieriebus.

Omnis modus dicitur imperfectus quandocumque ita est, quod aliquis modus desinit per aliam quantitatem quam per illam qua incipit; ut cum dicatur prima longa, altera brevis, altera longa et altera brevis.

Exemplum prime maneriei de modo perfecto :

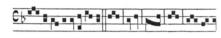

Latus.

Exemplum prime maneriei de imperfecto modo :

Fulminante.

Exemplum secunde de perfecto modo :

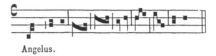

Angelus.

Exemplum secunde de imperfecto modo :

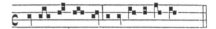

Et speravit. — In discantu moroso.

Exemplum tertie de perfecto modo :

Regnat.

TML model with musical examples.

```
Prima vero talis est: longa ante longam valet longam et brevem.
Secunda vero talis est: si multitudo brevium fuerit in aliquo loco, semper
debemus facere quod equipolleant longis.
Tertia vero talis est: si multitudo brevium fuerit in aliquo loco, quando
brevis plus appropinquat fini, tanto debet longior proferri.
Modus perfectus dicitur esse, quandocumque ita est quod aliquis modus desinit
per talem quantitatem vel per talem modum, sicuti per illam qua incipit.
Dicitur modus perfectus, ut dicatur prima longa, altera brevis, et altera
longa; et sic de singulis modis vel manieriebus.
Omnis modus dicitur imperfectus quandocumque ita est, quod aliquis modus
desinit per aliam quantitatem quam per illam qua incipit; ut cum dicatur prima
longa, altera brevis, altera longa et altera brevis.
Exemplum prime maneriei de modo perfecto:
[CSI:176,1; text: Latus.]
Exemplum prime maneriei de imperfecto modo:
[CSI:176,2; text: Fulminante.]
Exemplum secunde de perfecto modo:
[CSI:176,3; text: Angelus.]
Exemplum secunde de imperfecto modo:
[CSI:176,4; text: Et speravit. -- In discantu moroso.]
Exemplum tertie de perfecto modo:
[CSI:176,5; text: Regnat.]
```

TML encoding with musical examples.

Further information about the **Thesaurus Musicarum Latinarum** *may be obtained from* **Thomas Mathiesen**, *School of Music, Indiana University, Bloomington, IN 47405; tel. (812) 855-5471; e-mail: Mathiese@IUBACS.BITNET or Mathiese@UCS.Indiana.Edu.*

Rosamund McGuinness:
Register of Musical Data in London Newspapers, 1660-1800

Work on the *Register of Musical Data in London Newspapers, 1660-1800*, which has been reported in previous issues of *CM* (1991: 49, 1990: 136; 1987: 97; 1986: 56), is progressing steadily with the indexing of the material from 1660-1720 occurring simultaneously with the entry of material from 1720-1730.

The *Register* utilizes the *ORACLE* relational database management system. The relational database approach was taken to facilitate efficiency in querying the data: particular items may be held in common in a series of tables which are logically linked to each other. *ORACLE* was chosen because of its portability across mainframe, mini-, and microcomputer architectures. The related structured query language *SQL*Plus* is used for management and retrieval of information.

The notices about music found in London newspapers include precise information about concert life, music publishing, and instrument manufacture including indications of date and cost. Other topics that generate notices are the travels of individual musicians and composers, music instruction books, subscriptions, benefits, informal music-making (as, for example, in taverns and coffee houses), patronage, and education. The two extracts from the 1730's shown in the accompanying example extend to some of the most contentious and unusual aspects of the musical life of the time.

It is now possible to undertake interpretative work on the data up to 1720. That work is highlighting the value of the computer for the study of advertisements. Even at this early stage it has been possible to correct some of the misinterpretations of the period based upon incomplete data, *ad hoc* sampling or *a priori* judgments. For example, it has become evident that the usual explanations of increased wealth, social mobility and London's size go only part of the way in explaining the role of music in the metropolis at the time.

Ultimately it should be possible to examine the mechanisms by which taste was formed and in what ways the tastes so formed were a reflection of such agencies of information. Perceiving how the culture of music, commerce, and communication interacted in London during this period, we can begin to understand how this metropolis came to be an important urban center in the forefront of an important development, whereby culture with respect to music became commercialized and those in commerce were enabled and encouraged to seek culture.

Register of Musical Data in London Newspapers

From: the *Country Journal*; or, the *Craftsman*
Date: Saturday, April 28, 1733, p. 2

Whereas Daniel Wright, Instrument-maker in Holbourn, has published Lessons for the Harpsichord or Spinnet, under my Name and has asserted that they have been carefully corrected by me; this is to acquaint the Public, that those Lessons have been publish'd without my Knowledge or Consent; that many of them were not compos'd by me; and that those few which are mine, were composed many Years ago, and are very uncorrect. Beaufort Buildings, April 16, 1733, Maurice Green.

From: the *London Daily Post and General Advertiser*
Date: Wednesday, November 8, 1738, p. 1

A Grand Concert of Vocal and Instrumental Musick. Accompanied with the Harmony of a curious Machine of new Invention, called The Athenian University, or The Muses Paradise, now erected in the Great Room in Panton Street, will be performed there next Friday Evening. The Vocal by Mrs. Arne; the Oregan and Harpsichord by Mr. Digard. First Violin, by Mr. Brown; German Flute, by Mr. Ballycourt, and the rest of the Instruments by the best Hands from the Opera. The Beauty and Performances alone are worth the Notice of the Curious, being not only entertaining but edifying. It contains an Organ and an Harpsichord, an Orrery and an Air-Pump, a Barometer and Thermometer; also a curious Clock, which plays off the Organ, gives Motion to several Painted Figures, shews the Moon's Age and Phases, and by a Pair of Brass Globes solves several Problems in Astronomy and Geography; the Particulars of which are set forth in the Proposals, to be seen at most of the noted Coffee-houses in Town....Every Ticket entitles the Bearer to Two Concerts, or to Four Entertainments of the Machine's Performances, each of which will begin at Four o'clock every evening, except Wednesdays and Fridays; also to a chance of possessing the Machine and 253 l. per Annum Clear Rent in London....

Sample documents from the *Register of Musical Data in London Newspapers*.

When the database contents are complete, the developers foresee three methods of access. One is by online network access with custom-designed screens; one is by written request to the Music Department at Royal Holloway and Bedford New College; one is by CD-ROM with appropriate search software.

Rosamond McGuinness, *the director of this collaboration, is in the Department of Music, Royal Holloway and Bedford New College (University of London), Egham Hill, Egham, Surrey TW20 0EX, England; tel. +44 71/485-0209; fax +44 784/437520; e-mail: UHWM001@UK.AC. RHBNC.VAX.*

Thomas Griffin:
Musical References in the *Gazzetta di Napoli*

The *Gazzetta di Napoli* was a series of newssheets compiled weekly in the late seventeenth and early eighteenth centuries. This is a valuable source for dating musical events and new compositions precisely, for fixing the whereabouts of composers and performers, and for understanding musical patronage in this environment. Five hundred forty-six documents will be published both in print and on diskette by Fallen Leaf Press in 1993.

The associated program *Ricercar* provides a tool for rapid indexing and structured searches of ASCII texts, including these, stored on an MS DOS machine. Boolean searches are supported. *Ricercar*, which is available at nominal cost, can thus be used in studies involving management of large numbers of documents.

Thomas Griffin, *the editor of these references and the software designer, can be reached at 1255 Taylor St., #5, San Francisco, CA 94108; tel. (415) 921-4171; e-mail: tomg@iii.com. Fallen Leaf Press is located at 2419 Oregon St., Berkeley, CA 94705; tel. (510) 848-7805.*

Musical References in the *Gazzetta da Napoli*

17 *Napoli* - 4. Gennaro 1686. Num. 34

Si è poi recitata per due volte nel Regio Palazzo la famosa Opera intitolata l'Olimpia Vendicata, che fù da tutti gradita a maggior segno, così per la gran esquisitezza de Rappresentanti, come per la vaghezza delle scene. Fù grande il concorso delle Dame, e Cavalieri invitati da S.E. à quali fè dispensare con splendidezza reale, abondandissimi rinfreschi di canditi, e cioccolate. L'intessa Opera s'è cominciata a recitare nel Teatro di San Bartolomeo.

48 *Napoli* - 10. Agosto 1688. Num. 8

Il lunedì 2. del corrente il Sig. Prencipe di Sonnino, & il Sig. Marchese di Belvedere, solennezzorono li loro sponsalitij con concorso grande di Dame, e Cavalieri, a quali furono dispensati copiosissimi rinfreschi, e la sera gli si diede una bellissima serenata d'esquisiti musici.

62 *Napoli* - 17. Agosto 1694. Num. 44

Roma
Lunedì sera il Sig. Cardinale Ottoboni nel Giardino del Palazzo della Cancellaria con Altare fece fare per la Festa di S. Lorenzo sua Chiesa Titolare l'Oratorio molt sontuoso con sermone musica, e gran sinfonia di varietà d'Instromenti con intervento di molti Signori Cardinali, e Nobiltà.

74 *Napoli* - 8. Marzo 1695. Num. 10

Roma - 5. Marzo
Giovedì sera il Sig. Cardinale Ottoboni fece fare nel Seminario Romano un sontuoso Oratorio di Oloferne, e Giuditta cō bella comparsa di Musica, e Suonatori con invito, & intervento di molti Signori Cardinali.

Sample documents from Thomas Griffin's *Musical References in the Gazzetta da Napoli.*

The opera *Olimpia Vendicata* [#17] and the oratorio mentioned in #74 were set by Alessandro Scarlatti; the composer of the serenata mentioned in #48 is not known; the sinfonia described in #62 could have been by Corelli or Lulier.

John Howard:

RISM-US Music Manuscript Inventory

The RISM-US Music Manuscript Inventory represents the U.S. contribution to RISM Series A/II, a world-wide effort to document sources of music written in staff notation from the period of approximately 1600-1800. The project has been undertaken by the RISM-US Center for Musical Sources at Harvard University, under the auspices of the Joint Committee on RISM of the American Musicological Society and the Music Library Association, with major funding from the National Endowment for the Humanities.

The Center coordinates the cataloguing of music manuscripts within the United States and administers a database of bibliographic citations, including musical excerpts encoded with the *Plaine and Easie Code*. Data compiled is exported in machine-readable form to the RISM Zentralredaktion at Frankfurt-am-Main, Germany, for inclusion in the international RISM Series A/II database. The Center also oversees several independent data-processing activities, including preparation of printed or electronic output in response to scholarly enquiries and conversion of data to USMARC format for musical scores for export to the RLIN database of the Research Libraries Group.

Various software programs are used by the Center for its data-processing activities: *SPIRES* is employed for database management and the *SPIRES* procedural language for some output processing; a program to proofread encoded musical excerpts and convert data to *MuseData* format has been written by Brent Field of CCARH for the use of RISM; Leland Smith's *SCORE* program is used for preparation of EPS [*PostScript*] files for printed output; and Microsoft *Word* 5.0 and *Word for Windows* 2.0 are used for general document formatting [sample output is shown on p. 26].

Mediated access to the Center's database is provided by the Center's staff. Search requests can be submitted by letter or via e-mail to the address below. Search results can be returned as printed output, as an ASCII text file, or an ASCII *PostScript* file; encoded musical data can be provided separately in *Plaine and Easie*, *DARMS*, *MuseData*, or *SCORE* format. Broader access to the data is planned via the RLIN database system and through a planned CD-ROM product to be prepared by the RISM Zentralredaktion.

John B. Howard is at the RISM-US Center for Musical Sources, Music Building, Harvard University, Cambridge, MA 02138; tel. (617) 495-1624; fax (617) 496-4636; e-mail: RISM@harvarda.bitnet.

Felici, Alessandro 1742-1772
    6 Sonatas – cemb. C; D; F; c; G; B♭
[t.p., f. 1r:] Sei Sonate da Camera | per Cimbalo Solo, del' | Sig:r Alessandro Felici
Fiorenti:o
    Ms. 18.3q
    score: 30f
    22 x 29.5 cm
(f. 1v-5v:) all:o moderato, C, 2/4 - And:e, C, &C - Minuet Varazione, C, 3/4 — (f. 6v-11r:)
All:o, D, &C - And.e cantabile, G, &C - All:o spiritoso, D, 3/8 — (f. 11v-15r:) All:o
brilliante, F, &C - All:o assai, d, 3/4 - Presto, F, 3/4 — (f. 15v-19r:) All:o spiritoso, c, &C -
Presto, c, 3/8 — (f. 19v-24r:) Allegro, G, 3/4 - Andantino, g, 2/4 - Presto assai, G, 2/4 —
(f. 24v-29r:) And:e Cantabile, B♭, &C - All:o brilliante, B♭, 3/8 - Presto, B♭, 6/8

1.1. cemb. all:o moderato

2.1. cemb. All:o

3.1. cemb. All:o brillante

4.1. cemb. All:o spiritoso

5.1. cemb. Allegro

6.1. cemb. And:e Cantabile

keyb: cemb.
Ge: Minuet; Sonata da camera; Variazione
Binding: boards covered with pink marbled paper. – Music incipits transcribed as written
in the ms. – [cover title, on an engraved cartouche label:] SONATE DA CIMBALO | DEL
| SIG:R ALESSANDRO FELICI.
US BEm: MS 833
RISM: 00116673

RISM-US: A sample page of listings.

These incipits come from six keyboard sonatas by the Florentine composer Alessandro
Felici preserved in MS 833 (c.1750-75) at the University of California, Berkeley.

Kerala J. Snyder:
Cataloguing Sweden's Düben Collection

An extensive collection of manuscripts and prints assembled chiefly by Gustav Düben, Kapellmeister to the King of Sweden during the second half of the seventeenth century, was donated in 1732 to the University Library at Uppsala. The repertory comprises vocal and instrumental music, principally by German and Italian composers, with the main emphasis on sacred vocal music. The cataloguing project described here is a collaborative effort, begun in 1991, between members of the musicology department at Uppsala and at the Eastman School of Music. It is led by professors Kjellberg and Snyder and carried out by graduate students at both institutions.

The musicological aims of the Düben catalogue project are (1) to make this repertory more accessible for studies, editions, and performances; (2) to gain a broader understanding of the breadth of a large repertory whose peaks are currently understood to be represented by Schütz and Buxtehude; (3) to study the provenance, dating, and institutional context of the manuscripts themselves; (4) to gain insights into performance practice from the numerous performing parts; and (5) to facilitate the identification of anonymous works and the resolution of conflicting attributions.

A summary will be published in hard copy and the complete catalogue will be made available electronically, in a manner to be determined at the time of completion. In the meantime, we are furthering our educational goals for the students by providing them opportunities to work with both original sources and computer databases and to participate in international cooperation and exchange.

The first stage of our project involves entering into a database (*Paradox*) the basic information contained in earlier catalogues of the three parts of the repertory: vocal works in manuscript (Lindberg, 1946), instrumental works in manuscript (Kjellberg, 1968), and printed works (Mitjana and Davidsson, 1911-1951).

It was originally hoped that it would be possible either to draw upon or contribute to the RISM A/II catalogue of the manuscripts at Uppsala. Despite extensive cooperation on both sides this has proved impossible. That portion of the RISM catalogue is actually a list of works, conflating information from concordant sources into one entry per work, whereas our master database contains one entry per source item, with subsidiary linked tables tracking information on physical characteristics of the individual sources (collation, watermarks, handwriting, etc.) as well as musical characteristics of the works themselves, including incipits.

An encoding system for the incipits has not yet been selected, but Bengtsson's *Numericode*,[1] which the Swedish RISM office has been using successfully for over twenty years, is currently favored.

---

[1] *Numericode* represents diatonic (1-7) pitch and may optionally provide time values, also encoded numerically. A heading provides information on key (A-G) and mode (1 = major, 6 = minor), time signature, and first tone of the incipit.

References

Bengtsson, Ingmar. "Numericode—A Code System for Thematic Incipits," *Svensk tidskrift för musikforskning*, 49 (1967), 5-40.

Grusnick, Bruno. "Die Dübensammlung: Ein Versuch ihrer chronologischen Ordnung," *Svensk tidskrift för musikforskning*, 46 (1964), 27-82; 48 (1966), 63-186.

Kjellberg, Erik. "Kungliga musiker i sverige under stormakstiden: Studier kring deras organisation, verksamheter och status, ca. 1620 - ca. 1720." 2 vols. Ph.D. dissertation, Uppsala University, 1979.

Lindberg, Folke. "Katalog över Dübensamlingen in Uppsala universitets bibliotek: Vokalmusik i handskrift." Typescript, Uppsala, 1946.

Mitjana, Raphael, and Äke Davidsson. *Catalogue critique et descriptif des imprimés de musique des XVIe et XVIIe siècles, conservés à la bibliothèque de l'Université Royale d'Uppsala.* 3 vols. Uppsala: Almquist and Wiksell, 1911-1951.

Rudén, Jan Olof. "Vattenmärken och Musikforskning: Presentation och Tillämpning av en Dateringsmetod på musikalier i handskrift i Uppsala Universitetsbiblioteks Dübensamling." 2 vols. Licentiate thesis, Uppsala University, 1968.

Snyder, Kerala J. *Dietrich Buxtehude: Organist in Lübeck.* New York: Schirmer Books, 1987.

....

Kerala J. Snyder *can be reached at the Eastman School of Music, University of Rochester, 26 Gibbs Street, Rochester, NY 14604; tel. (716) 274-1458; e-mail: KSYR@dbl.cc.rochester.edu.*
Erik Kjellberg *can be reached at the Institute of Musicology, Uppsala University, Sweden; fax: +46 18 12 09 54; e-mail: MUSEK@strix.udac.uu.se.*

Paul R. Laird:

International Inventory of *Villancico* Texts

This project [described in *CM 1991*, p. 45] continues as a coordinated international effort to establish bibliographic control over villancico texts found in printed sources and manuscripts. In May 1992 the database held incipits and other information for more than 5,600 villancicos from Iberian and Latin American sources. Over the past year the study of textual concordances and dissemination patterns has been a central task. So far more than 700 definite and possible concordances have been identified.

After presentations involving the database at the International Musicological Society Congress (April 3-9, 1992) in Madrid, Spain, and the conference *After Columbus: The Voyage Continues (May 21-23)* at California Polytechnic State University, the database now has correspondents in Còrdoba, Granada, Madrid, Salamanca, Seville, Valladolid, and Zaragoza, Spain; as well as Argentina (Buenos Aires); France (Paris); Great Britain (London); Guatemala (Guatemala City); Mexico (Mexico City); and Venezuela (Caracas). Researchers at these locations will be providing incipits from printed and manuscript villancicos, and in return will be provided with textual concordances from the database.

Paul R. Laird is at the Lamont School of Music, University of Denver, 7111 Montview Blvd., Denver, CO 80220; tel. (303) 871-6920; e-mail: PLAIRD@DUCAIR.BITNET or PLAIRD @DU.EDU. David Martìnez serves as assistant director.

Graham Pont, Nigel Nettheim:

The Notation of Baroque Music: A Database of Scanned Images

A lexicon of images, extracted from manuscript and early printed sources, is being created in order to facilitate comparison of sources. The images, generally measuring about one square inch, are optically scanned and stored as bit-maps. A custom program utilizes accompanying documentation concerning the composer, date of the source, genre of the music, notational category, and so forth, to facilitate historical research. The defining dates of the materials are from *c.* 1600 to 1770.

In a pilot phase, extracts from 21 representative works, from Caccini (1600) to J. S. Bach (1723), have been captured, stored, and surveyed. Each image is stored and recalled by number. The earliest images to be processed are shown in the accompanying illustrations. The examples of Font A come from Florentine secular vocal music (Peri's and Caccini's *Euridice)* and of Font B from Roman sacred music (Emilio Cavalieri's *Rappresentatione di anima e di corpo*); both sources were printed in the year 1600.

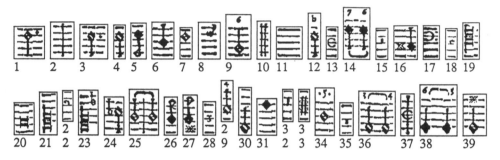

Font A: images from *Euridice* (1600).

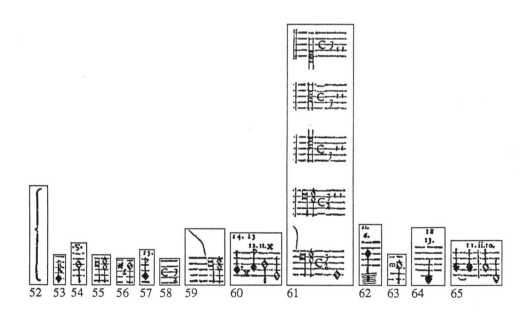

Font B: images from *La rappresentatione di anima e di corpo* (1600).

Graham Pont, *principal investigator, and* **Nigel Nettheim**, *programming consultant, are both at the Centre for Liberal and General Studies, University of New South Wales, PO Box 1, Kensington, NSW 2033, Australia; tel. +61 2/697-2367; fax +61 2/313 7682; e-mail: pont @cumulus.csd.unsw.oz.au and nigel@cumulus.csd.unsw.oz.au.*

Using Networks

in Musical Research

Tutorial:

Using Networks in Musical Research

The electronic interconnection of computers supports an ever-growing number of user services. This article is concerned with three of them—individual mail, group digests and archives, and anonymous file transfers. The information we provide, which has been compiled primarily from experience and online documentation, is as general as we can make it; the specifics may vary according to the systems software in use at the user's end.

Measures of Data and Data Transmission

A great range of hardware and software systems facilitate access to information originating in a different location from that of the user. There are numerous steps in the process of data transfer; the exact number depends on the systems in use. Few of the component processes utilize recognized standards. A general understanding of the variables involved can be helpful in configuring one's own environment for optimum access to the desired networks.

Networks differ according to the methods used to transport information from one location to another. The standard measure of information in the computer world is the byte. In computer memory, a byte contains eight bits. In modem transmissions, however, ten-bit packets are normally used. The first bit is a start bit and the last a stop bit. Some systems handle seven data bits (instead of eight) by adding a "parity bit" (for error checking) before the stop bit; others add a second stop bit. While some network connections (*e.g.*, to CompuServe) require the user to accommodate a specific configuration (*e.g.*, even parity), this is normally handled automatically by the software.

A measure of transmission speed, the so-called baud rate, is actually a measure of the number of signal changes per second supported by the transmission hardware. Since modern transmission techniques allow a signal change to represent multiple bits, the bits-per-second rate (used below) can be several times the baud rate. The baud rate may be the same as or significantly less than the bps rate. Modems conforming to the V.*22bis* format provide a baud rate of one-quarter the bps (*i.e.*, 2400 bps = 600 baud), and so forth. V.*32bis* modems handle up to 14,400 bps by packing six to a signal and sending 2,400 signals per second. V.*42bis* modems provide an additional compression technique. The file transfer procedures described later benefit from the use of relatively sophisticated modems. Compatibility issues must be explored by the user.

Networks available for Academic Use

Over the past fifteen years a number of widely used families of academic networks have been established. Each has originated in a different specific hardware environment, and these diverse environments continue to cast a shadow on current methods of access and operation. Each has separate addressing formats.

The BITNET Family

BITNET ("Because It's Time Network") supports mail, list servers, and archives but does not permit remote login. It is organized as a point-to-point network: transmissions are sent in packets of data through a series of mainframes (or "gateways") until they reach their destination. Each gateway handles the data according to parameters that affect transmissions speed and the eventual form in which the data arrive.

Started as a cooperative academic network in 1981, BITNET was merged in 1989 with CSNET and officially became CREN (Corporation for Regional and Educational Networking). EARNNET, the European Academic Research Network serving Europe, the Middle East, and North Africa, and NetNorth, serving Canada, use the same networking protocols as BITNET. BITNET has been and remains a potent force in academic networking. It serves many university computing facilities and individual users of personal computers. Its association with the archiving facilities called list- [or mail-] servers is especially strong. As an exclusively academic and research network, BITNET has been able to concentrate on the needs of this community.

The Internet Family

The Internet is a supernetwork of more than 1000 networks serving universities, businesses, and government research facilities worldwide. Its operation extends to almost 600,000 host computers. The backbone of the Internet is another network, the (US) National Science Foundation Network (NSFNET). The Internet is the fastest of the existing networks, but exactly how fast depends upon the local environment. The Internet is especially heavily used by researchers using workstations with UNIX operating systems. Use of the Internet is more flexible than that of BITNET; the services available—electronic mail, remote login to and file transfer from distant hosts—are more extensive.

The TCP/IP protocol used by the Internet is system-independent. Internet addressing supports connections between machines with different operating systems (*e.g.*, PCs running MS DOS and workstations running under UNIX). Macintoshes can access the

Internet and when running *MacTCP* can function directly as nodes. *TCP* stands for Transmission Control Protocol, which provides the *transport layer* of communication. *IP* stands for the Internet Protocol, which links networks together. Preceding these is an *applications layer* which relies on FTP (file transfer protocol).

A PC or Macintosh remotely logged in to the Internet can emulate UNIX terminals and run UNIX programs with appropriate software. This significantly expands the range of capabilities available to the user through the listserve option offered by BITNET. At the same time, it requires knowledge of a small set of UNIX commands.

JANET

JANET is the UK's Joint Academic Network. It provides mail, file transfer, news, and information and is maintained at *jnt@rutherford.ac.uk*. Although it has gateways to the Internet, EUnet, and BITNET, it has become increasingly reliant on the Internet.

The UUCP Family

UUCP [UNIX-to-UNIX Copy Program] was originally designed to work on telephone lines. A group of systems using this protocol form a loosely organized network serving Europe and North America and operating at range of speeds (1200 to 11,000 bps). The enabling software has been implemented on many other platforms. It works by a technique called polling: one machine canvasses another at regular intervals for messages. UUCP supports mail and Usenet news.

The UUCP protocol is used by EUnet (the European UNIX Network), a cooperative network serving members of the EEC and Scandinavia. Some EUnet sites can be reached by Internet-style addresses [support is available from *glenn@eu.net*]. For those who are unable to accept these, the backbone site *mcsun* can relay messages to most countries of northern, western, and central Europe. The format is *mcsun!host!user*.

JUNET (the Japanese UNIX Network), serving research institutions in Japan, was originally analogous in its operation to UUCP but is now converting to the TCP/IP protocol used by the Internet.

Commercial Networks

Commercial networks such as ATTMail, CompuServe, MCIMail, and SprintMail provide electronic mail services as part of a basic package provided for a modest monthly fee. They now provide access to academic networks. CompuServe also provides access to several dozen electronic forums on music (especially MIDI) software. Directories can be searched by product name.

Commercial Network Access

Those who do not have access to a university or commercial host computer for electronic communications and do not wish to have the kind of packaged services offered by commercial networks may be able to find commercial services that will provide academic network access as an exclusive service for a monthly fee. In the San Jose, California, area, for example, Netcom is such a public-access provider. [Netcom's fax number is (408) 241-9145; tel. 554-8649; enquirers may also logon as "guest" at (415) 241-9760 or (415) 424-0131)]. General Electric sells access to AppleLink. E-mail access is available through the address format < *user* > *@applelink.apple.com*. [Material shown in pointed brackets is generic; the user must substitute specific information.]

Network Services (1): Mail

Software to manage electronic mail is available from many vendors and academic computing centers. In order to send and receive mail, one needs an electronic address. Each network uses a different addressing format.

On most networks electronic addresses have two essential components—a user identifier ("user") and a site identifier ("host"). On BITNET and the Internet they are connected by the sign "@".

When communications are sent over a network, they pass from node to node. When it is necessary to go from one network to another, they must pass through a super-node or gateway. Under some circumstances, such as that of needing to specify a gateway, there may be three components to the address. In this instance, the user and host identifiers are separated by the sign " % " and the nodes are separated by the sign "@". UUCP addresses use the sign "!" (called a "bang") as a separator.

Host Names

While host ID names in BITNET are usually in a simple (often eight-character) format (frequently concatenating a university acronym and a machine or operating system name), the Internet host name has multiple parts that reflect a hierarchy ("domain addressing") and, except between hosts in the UK (when the order after the "@" is reversed), these are usually given from the most finite unit, such as a specific computer, to the most general, such as a country code, *e.g.*, *VAX.OXFORD.AC.UK*. In network-ese, these subcomponents are the "machine" (VAX), the "campus" (OXFORD), and the "domain" (AC). The academic domain in the US is normally *edu*. Users with access to both

BITNET and the Internet can sometimes use a common ID on both, but host names are likely to be significantly different from network to network. Data can be sent into BITNET from other networks by appending to the host name the expression ".BITNET". No such extension is required to send mail into the Internet.

Domains

Besides the academic domain (*edu* or *ac*), some common Internet domains are *com* (commercial), *gov* (government), and *net* (network). The Internet is said to use "domain-style" addressing, in which the institutional name is a "submask".

Country Codes

Country names are often suffixed to domain names. Some common country codes are:

au	Australia	*it*	Italy
ca	Canada	*jp*	Japan
cn	China	*kr*	Korea
de	Germany	*no*	Norway
fi	Finland	*su*	Russia
fr	France	*uk*	United Kingdom
il	Israel	*us*	United States

[A complete list of country codes (216 items) is given in Kehoe, pp. 95-8.]

One pitfall of electronic addressing is that certain alphanumeric concatenations, because they defy any sense of euphony or linguistic logic, are easily misconstrued. For example, we write fairly often to the address *JMP100@DE0HRZ1A*, in which the possibility of interchanging lower-case "l"s with numerical "1"s and upper-case "O"s with numerical "0"s is plainly evident. In some UNIX and mainframe systems the distinction between upper- and lower-case letters is essential, while in others it is irrelevant.

As electronic messages travel along a route of nodes, some systems return a "milestone" message for each node through which the message passes. By watching these messages, the sender can verify that the message has been delivered. Some large computing facilities have the capability to switch processing of outgoing mail from one machine to another. The headers of arriving mail, elements of which are acquired in transit, may contain addresses that are not serviceable for mail dispatch [a few CCARH correspondents have experienced this phenomenon for reasons that are beyond our control]. A "Do as I say, not as I do" practice may pertain.

Sample Address Formats

For the sake of illustration, we have invented a hypothetical user, Jane Doe. She uses a host computer code-named Star at an academic institution called Galaxy. She can receive mail via BITNET, EARN, the Internet, JANET, and UUCP. She is also user 12345,678 on CompuServe and MCIMail [the comma is changed to a period when sending messages from outside the system]. Here is how mail might be sent from an external network to her various mailboxes [we assume no upper/lower-case permutations between addresses]:

> *BITNET*   *JaneDoe@galaxy.bitnet*
> *Internet*   *JaneDoe@star.galaxy.edu*
> *UUCP*   *uunet!galaxy!JaneDoe*

If Jane Doe is based in the UK, messages might be addressed to:

> *Janet* [from outside UK]   *JaneDoe@star.galaxy.ac.uk*
> *Janet* [from inside UK]   *JaneDoe@galaxy.star*

To reach her mailboxes on commercial networks in the US, the formats would be:

> *CompuServe*   *12345.678@compuserve.com*
> *MCIMail*   *12345.678@mcimail.com*

If mailing from a commercial to an academic network, the network name may need to be prefixed:

> *INTERNET:JaneDoe@star.galaxy.edu*

When electronic mail crosses from one network to another, the host names of backbone nodes or gateways may accrue to the message. Some important gateways and their electronic identifications are these:

> *BITNET-UUCP*:   *psuvax1* [=Pennsylvania State University]
> *Internet-USENET*:   *berkeley.edu* [=University of California, Berkeley]
> *UUCP-Internet*   *UUNET* [=Arlington, VA]

Registered UUCP hosts can receive mail from other networks via the host *uunet.uu.net*.

IP and FidoNet Addresses

The TCP/IP protocol associated with the Internet requires that every networked machine have a unique numerical designation in four parts, none of which may exceed the number 256, *e.g.*, 128.127.50.12. These numerical identifiers may be needed for remote login but they are not necessary for mail and list access. IP addresses are assigned by the DNN Network Information Center (*hostmaster@nic.dnn.mil*).

FidoNet, which operates within the Internet, utilizes a sub-numbering system of the machine node such that if Jane Doe were said to be on the node 5:6/7.8, her address would be *JaneDoe@p5.f6.n7.z8.fidonet.edu*.

Network Services (2): Digests and Archives

In addition to their value in interpersonal and group communications, networks have facilitated the creation of two new forms of scholarly communication—research digests and electronic archives. Both spring from mainframe computer software support for mailing lists, but they serve different practical purposes and utilize different methods of dissemination. In both cases it is necessary to register as a subscriber in order to receive materials.

Research digests serve a multitude of purposes. Many were founded along the line of bulletin boards, where observations may be informally shared. Digests and archives must be maintained by a moderator, who assumes the duties of maintaining a list of subscribers, reading materials submitted for redistribution, setting policy guidelines, and redistributing those messages selected for the purpose.

In principle, digests are automatically mailed electronically to all subscribers, while subscribers to archives receive only listings of new accessions; they must then request the specific files of interest. Digests accept unsolicited contributions, while archives may contain only materials provided on assignment. Either kind of service may be the exclusive province of members of a particular society. The *Music Research Digest* moderated by Stephen Page, exemplifies the digest type of publication. Anyone may subscribe and anyone may contribute. The materials are first archived at Oxford University, where Page completed a D. Phil. in 1988. From Oxford they are distributed to British subscribers and sent to a secondary host at the University of Pennsylvania (Philadelphia, PA), from which they are redistributed to readers outside the UK.

The *Thesaurus Musicarum Latinarum* [see pp. 18-20] exemplifies the archive model. A database of electronic encodings of medieval and Renaissance writings in Latin on music theory is steadily accruing. Anyone may access the materials, but contributions are carefully planned and twice verified before deposit. The project has been designed and is headed by Thomas Mathiesen of Indiana University.

Increasingly, hybrid models are appearing. *EthnoFORUM*, a service of the Society for Ethnomusicology, provides both an electronic digest (*Ethnomusicology Research Digest*) mailed automatically to *bona fide* subscribers and an archive of extended research and teaching materials available only to members of the society. *ERD* is clearly structured and carefully edited. Appearing biweekly, it contains job announcements, dissertation abstracts, and research reports. The service is moderated by Karl Signell at the University of Maryland, Baltimore County (Catonsville, MD).

A number of electronic services has also been put in place by the Society for Music Theory. Moderated by Lee Rothfarb at Harvard University, the SMT service consists of one main conference, touching on diverse subject areas of music theory, and a bibliographical search service involving a database of citations to articles and reviews published in the major music-theoretical journals. A database of musical examples (appearing primarily in journals of music theory), created by Justin London (*jlondon@carleton.edu*), is also accessible. The SMT services are primarily for members of the society, but subscription is open to others upon request (*smt-editor@husc. harvard.edu* or *smt-editor@husc.bitnet*).

Music scholars may find value in a number of digests and archives that are concerned more broadly with the humanities. A number of European countries have established state-subsidized services of this kind. *HUMBUL* [Humanities Bulletin] in the United Kingdom is an especially successful example in that it is both clearly organized, easy to use, and extremely capacious in its holdings. Subscribers passively receive a listing of recently entered items [conference announcements, vacancies lists, publication notices, copies of electronic publications, including *MRD*, etc.]. To receive the actual items listed, they must actively request them. This model has the virtue of not filling one's mailbox with material that may seem irrelevant. Stuart Lee is the current moderator of *HUMBUL*; its home base is at Oxford University. [In the accompanying illustration on p. 41 we have left intact some of the non-translatable and wholly irrelevant UNIX codes, because they typify the sometimes imperfect nature of cross-platform communications.]

Humbul

<05050505>STOP PRESS
<050505>RECENT ADDITIONS TO HUMBUL
(For Information on how to download sections see section **A2**)

Date	<05>Section Updated	Topic
6 Jul 92<05>**C2**	-Conferences Overseas<05>	ACL, 21-3 April 1993, Utrecht
6 Jul 92<05>**P5**	-Ongoing Research<0505>	Survey of Comp. Ling. Courses
6 Jul 92<05>**C1**	-Conferences UK<0505>	CAL 93, 5-8 April 1993, York
6 Jul 92<05>**B1**	-General News<0505>	Ethics Starter Kit
6 Jul 92<05>**H8a**	-CONTENTS News<0505>	Galatians Bibliography
6 Jul 92<05>**J8**	-JANET Services<0505>	SCHOLAR - Online NLP service
6 Jul 92<05>**B2a**	-Books and Reports<0505>	Elizabethan Conference Report
6 Jul 92<05>**L3**	-Situations Vacant<0505>	Anthropology Vacancy, Oxford
6 Jul 92<05>**L3**	-Situations Vacant<0505>	Linguistics Vacancy, Leicester Polytechnic
6 Jul 92<05>**C2**	-Conferences Overseas<05>	Euralex 92, 4-9 August, Tampere
6 Jul 92<05>**C2**	-Conferences Overseas<05>	9th Brazilian Symposium, 5-8 October 1992, Rio

Date<0505>Section Updated<050505>Topic

6 Jul 92<05>**I8**	-Major Projects<0505>	New Edition of Directory of Scholarly E-serials
<05050505 0505>and Journals		
6 Jul 92<05>**K8**	-Courses<050505>	College Certificate in Computer Applications, RHBNC,
<05050505 0505>London		
8 Jun 92<05>**J8**	-JANET Services<0505>	Medieval List
8 Jun 92<05>**C2**	-Conferences Overseas<05>	ACM on Hypertext, 30 Nov-4 Dec 1992, Milan
4 Jun 92<05>**J8**	-JANET Services<0505>	Mark Twain List
4 Jun 92<05>**L3**	-Situations Vacant<0505>	British National Corpus Job

A sample *HUMBUL* index mailing. *HUMBUL* distributes listings of this kind to its subscribers. Subscribers who wish to read selected materials send a message identifying the appropriate (archived) section. In this edited version of a *HUMBUL* mailing, section designations are in bold face and bracketed codes [non-translatable UNIX] are in small type. The message "*GET L3 SECTION HUMBUL*" will elicit all the vacancy listings; the message "*GET C2 SECTION HUMBUL*" will retrieve all the overseas conference postings, and so forth.

List Servers

The retrieval of all of these materials requires access to a list server. A list server is a mail-response program (called *LISTSERV*) set up on a host mainframe. When a user sends it a request, it will return a response automatically. *LISTSERV* can function in (1) mail mode, (2) command job mode, and (3) interactive mode. Each mode has a different syntax; we deal here only with mail mode. A list server understands and responds to only a few commands, such as *HELP* (send information), *INDEX* (send a directory of holdings), and *SEND* (send a file). In mail mode each line is read as a separate command. Message files need only contain one line, although if multiple actions are sought, a separate line must be provided for each command. The exact components of a message will vary from list to list, although the overall vocabulary is limited and there is much overlap. The first element is frequently an active verb, such as *SUBSCRIBE* or *GET*; the command to leave a list is usually *SIGNOFF*. We have summarized the main commands relating to list servers on the tables following [pp. 44-7].

A list server has its own user-ID. Very often it is "*LISTSERV*". The automatically maintained subscriber list also has a user ID. Commonly it is the list name followed by "-L" (*e.g.*, TML-L or MLA-L). The moderator has a user ID. There may be a fourth user ID for a file that receives contributions. The host names may all be identical. In order to use a list server, it is usually necessary to keep track of several addresses and to understand when each is appropriate. Most moderators are glad to provide help.

An additional reason for maintaining one's own file of addresses is the fact that many archives may reside in more than one host and be accessible from more than one network. The addresses will vary with the hosts and the commands will vary with the network.

Some additional *LISTSERV* commands are *INFO GENINTRO* (send introductory material), *REVIEW* <*listname*>*-L* (send the names of other subscribers), and *SET* <*listname*>*-L CONCEAL* (conceal my name in the subscriber list). Users of an IBM VM/CMS system (operating in interactive mode) should preface all *LISTSERV* commands with the words *TELL LISTSERV*, *e.g.*

TELL LISTSERV@AUVM SUB MUSIC-L Jane Doe

The VAX VMS (non-interactive) alternative to TELL is SEND.

To request a name change, you may send a *SUBSCRIBE* command to the list or a personal note to the moderator. To change an electronic address, you may send a *SIGN OFF* command for the old address and a *SUBSCRIBE* command for the new address. Additional capabilities are described in the document elicited with the command *INFO*

DATABASE on most list servers. File logs may be ordered by month (*MM*) and year (*YY*). For example, the *TML* has a log of messages arranged by year. These can be retrieved with the command *GET TML-L LOG91*. When the automatic *REPLY* command available on some systems is used, the response will automatically be distributed to all subscribers. Personal messages should instead be sent to the moderator.

Digests maintained on the Internet can require more administration than those on BITNET, and more addresses are therefore likely to be necessary in order to use them. Tasks concerned with subscription, for instance, may be directed to an address with the suffix "—*request*".

Network Services (3): File Transfer Protocol (FTP)

The purpose of the *file transfer protocol* (FTP) is to enable transfer of files between hosts over the Internet. It is especially popular for its ability to provide access to remote hosts. FTP is used interactively. It differentiates between client computers and host computers. By allowing remote login, FTP makes subscription lists unnecessary. The FTP world is something of a free-for-all, in which any user in possession of the right addressing information can search computers around the world for files designated for public access. The kinds of files that are available through FTP range from product postings and user comments about software and hardware to entire programming environments, software documentation, and actual programs. Some programs in FTP archives are shareware: users who plan to use them regularly are required to pay a modest fee to the developer. A great many cost-free programs are available by FTP. For these, only minimal support is generally provided.

Telnet and FTP

Telnet is a terminal emulation program which allows one to logon to a remote machine via the Internet. Through *Telnet* it is possible to read one's mail while away from home and to execute programs on a remote host.

FTP provides independent support for remote login. The commands required to open a session are system-dependent. Since FTP is interactive, it is necessary to *logon* (in some cases the user name "anonymous" is accepted with password such as "guest" or the user's e-mail address). User access is not as anonymous as it may appear: FTP hosts keep track of the e-mail addresses of past clients. For a full list of commands, type *help* at any FTP prompt.

Summary of Address and Command Information

No.	A List Name, Host Address	B Moderator's name, personal e-mail address	C Address for subscription, file retrieval	D Command to subscribe	E Command to leave list
1	Center for Electronic Texts in the Humanities (CETH) 169 College Avenue New Brunswick, NJ 08903	Annelies Hoogcarspel CETH@ZODIAC.BITNET ceth@zodiac.rutgers.edu	*Bitnet:* LISTSERV@PUCC *Internet:* LISTSERV@pucc.princeton.edu	SUBSCRIBE CETH *Jane Doe* (to 1C)	SIGN OFF CETH Jane Doe SIGN OFF CETH Jane Doe (to 1C)
2	Ethnomusicology Research Digest (ERD) Dept. of Turkish Music University of Maryland Baltimore County Catonsville, MD 21228	Karl Signell SIGNELL@UMDD.BITNET	*Bitnet:* LISTSERV@UMDD.BITNET *Internet:* LISTSERV@UMDD.UMD.EDU *ftp* INFO.UMD.EDU ip 128.8.10.29	SUBSCRIBE ETHMUS-L *Jane Doe* (to 2C)	SIGNOFF ETHMUS-L Jane Doe UNS ETHMUS-L Jane Doe (to 2C)
3	Humanities Bulletin Board (HUMBUL) CTI Centre for Literature 13 Banbury Road Oxford University Oxford OX2 6NN, England	Stuart Lee STUART@VAX.OX.AC.UK	*Internet:* HUMBUL @VAX.OXFORD.AC.UK	SUB HUMBUL *Jane Doe* (to 3C)	
4	Music Research Digest (MRD) Computing Centre Oxford University Oxford UK [moderator lives in London]	UK only: Stephen Page music-research-request @prg.ox.ac.uk US et al.: Peter Marvit music-research-request @cattell.psych.upenn.edu	From UK only: archive-server @uk.ac.oxford.prg From elsewhere: archive-server @cattell.psych.upenn.edu *ftp* [UK] comlab.oc.ac.uk *ftp* [US] cattell.psych.upenn.edu	Send message to 4B	Send message to 4B
5	Thesaurus Musicarum Latinarum (TML) School of Music Indiana University Bloomington, IN 47405	Thomas Mathiesen MATHIESE @IUBACS.BITNET	*Bitnet:* LISTSERV@IUBVM *Internet:* LISTSERV@IUBVM.UCS. INDIANA.EDU ip 129.79.1.10	SUBSCRIBE TML-L *Jane Doe* (to 5C)	SIGNOFF TML-L (to 5C)

Summary, cont.

No.	(A) List Name	F Command to retrieve general information	G Command to retrieve an index of available files	H Command to retrieve a file	I Address to which to send contributions
1	**CETH**	INFO GENINTRO [for Listserv] (1C)	INDEX CETH (1C)	GET CETH LOGYYMM (1C)	By request only
2	**ERD; EthnoFORUM**	GET WELCOME INFO INFO GENINTRO (2C)	INDEX ETHMUS-L (2C)	GET ETHMUS-L *filetype* [news, jobs, discussion] (2C)	ETHMUS-L@UMDD.BITNET [digest] SIGNELL@UMDD.BITNET [files for archive]
3	**HUMBUL**	GET A2 SECTION HUMBUL (3C)	GET T SECTION HUMBUL (3C)	GET *filename* SECTION HUMBUL (3C)	HUMBUL@VAX.OXFORD.AC.UK
4	**MRD**	HELP DIGEST (4C)	INDEX DIGEST (4C)	SEND DIGEST (4C) With FTP [US] look in: /pub/Music-Research	Music-Research @prg.oxford.ac.uk OR Music-Research %prg.oxford.ac.uk @nsfnet-relay.ac.uk
5	**TML**	GET INTRO TEXT TML-L (5C)	INDEX TML-L [then] GET *16th* FILELIST TML-L (5C)	GET *VITARSN TEXT* TML-L (5C)	By request only

Key: Command elements in italics are variables. Designations in parentheses refer to addresses in individual cells in this table. The *TML* file lists (5G) are organized by century; file names (5H) are by author/treatise designation. Apart from *ERD*, which is by subscription (2D), *EthnoFORUM* archival files (2H; see 2I) are for retrieval by SEM members only.

Other List Servers related to Music

Name	Moderator	Subscriptions	Contributions	Host
All Music (2) ALLMUSIC [discussion] AMUSIC-D [digest]	Mike Karolchik American University Washington, DC U6183@WVNVM.WVNET.EDU	SUBSCRIBE ALLMUSIC *Jane Doe*	ALLMUSIC@AUVM.BITNET	LISTSERV@AUVM.BITNET LISTSERV@AUVM.AUVM.EDU
Chinese Music	Theodore Kwok University of Hawaii Law Library 2525 Dole Street Honolulu, HA 96822 tedk@uhunix.bitnet tedk@uhunix.uhcc.hawaii.edu	SUBSCRIBE ACMR-L *Jane Doe*	ACMR-L@UHCCVM.BITNET	LISTSERV@UHCCVM.BITNET
Early Music: records, books, musical events, sources, and technical matters	Gerhard Gonter University of Vienna Vienna, Austria GONTER@AWIWUW11.BITNET	SUBSCRIBE EARLYM-L *Jane Doe*	EARLYM-L@AEARN.BITNET	LISTSERV@AEARN.BITNET
Electronic Music (2) EMUSIC-L [Unedited] EMUSIC-D [Digest]	Eric Harnden American University Washington, DC EHARNDEN@AUVM.AUVM.EDU	SUBSCRIBE EMUSIC-L and/or SUBSCRIBE EMUSIC-D *Jane Doe*	EMUSIC-L@AUVM.BITNET EMUSIC-D@AUVM.BITNET	LISTSERV@AUVM.BITNET LISTSERV@AUVM.AUVM.EDU
International Council for Traditional Music: Study Group on Computer-Aided Research Newsletter: **INFO**	Helmut Schaffrath Universität Essen, FB 4-Musik- Postfach, W-4300 Essen 1, Germany JMP100@DE0HRZ1A.BITNET	Send message to moderator	Send to moderator	Not a list server

Other List Servers, cont.

Name	Moderator	Subscriptions	Contributions	Host
Music Library Association	**Ralph Papakhian** Indiana University Library Bloomington, IN 47405 (812) 855-2970 PAPAKHI@IUBVM.BITNET papakhi@iubvm.ucs.indiana.edu	Everyone welcome SUBSCRIBE MLA-L *Jane Doe*	Mainly from members; others should query first	LISTSERV@IUBVM.BITNET
Mu[sic]TeX users	**Werner Icking** GMD Schloss Birlinghoven P.O. Box 1316 D-5205 Sankt Augustin, Germany +49 2241/14-2443 icking@gmd.de	Send message to mutex-request@stolaf. edu	From users	ftp.gmd.de
Society for Music Theory	**Lee Rothfarb** Department of Music Harvard University Cambridge, MA 02138 rothfarb@husc.bitnet rothfarb@husc.harvard.edu	Discussion group access and bibliographical searches available only to members	From members primarily; others may request access	

FTP Logon for the *TML*

VMS Command:
$ ftp 129.79.1.10
[Your mainframe's address will be displayed]
 Connection opened
 Using 8-bit bytes.
220-FTPSRV2 at IUBVM.UCS.INDIANA.EDU, 23:18:33 EST THURSDAY 01/10/91
220 Connection will close if idle for more than 5 minutes
Name: (129.79.1.10: mathiese): **tml-ftp**
331 Send password please.
Password: **themulat**
332-TML-FTP logged in; no working directory defined
332 to access TML-FTP 191, send 'ACCOUNT minidisk-password'
quote acct themulat
230 Working directory is TML-FTP 191 (ReadOnly)

FTP session logon. This sample computer-user dialogue initiates a session aimed at reading files in the *Thesaurus Musicarum Latinarum*. The material in bold-face type must be supplied by the user.

To search directories on a remote host, the user must provide the name of the host machine on which the directories reside. Directories maintained by Jane Doe (and many others) might be accessed with the command *ftp star.galaxy.edu*. Once access to the remote host is established, an FTP prompt will be provided. Some possible commands with which to respond are:

> *dir*   list files in the current directory
> *cd*   change directory
> *get*   make a host file available to the client
> *put*   send a client file to the host

File Format Conversion

The process of downloading files from archives and list servers can be complicated by file size and file format. Communications programs have diverse upper limits [often under 100K] on the amount of ASCII text they can handle at one go. Because of limits imposed by BITNET, the maximum file size in the *TML* is 300K. To save storage in the host computer, archived files may be compressed. The UNIX extension ".*Z*", the DOS extension ".*zip*" and the Macintosh extensions ".*CPT*" and ".*SIT*" indicate that stored files are compressed. Under some circumstances it is desirable to change the data format prior to the use of the command *get*, and it is often necessary to decompress or re-convert the material after receipt. The specific commands required are dependent on the software in the client system.

Using FTP on a PC

PC users may use FTP if all the essential enabling tools are in place. These include a computer with a TCP/IP communications card, Internet access, and an address (either alphabetic or numerical) for the host system. The names of relevant directories and files on the host can speed search and retrieval. We provide on the facing page a sample dialogue demonstrating how to interact with the *TML*'s host system using FTP.

Through FTP it is also possible to gain access to DOS [and other operating system] files and applications on a remote host. PC implementations of TCP are card-specific.

Using FTP on a Mac

Macintosh users may wish to explore several options for terminal emulation. The program *NCSA Telnet* is distributed from some archives as freeware. Alternatively *MacIP*, which consists of two disks and is accompanied by a manual, is available from *ccrma.stanford.edu*. Both packages provide *Telnet* for terminal emulation and FTP software; each requires that either the Macintosh has an Ethernet card connected to the Internet or that the Macintosh is on an Appleshare network with an Appleshare—TCP/IP bridge. [Ethernet cards cost several hundred US dollars, and bridge software is several times more costly.]

Using FTP without the Internet

A query program named *archie*, designed at McGill University to enable users to browse through lists of the holdings of more than 1000 anonymous FTP sites worldwide, is accessible via interactive *Telnet* (and the UNIX equivalent *rlogin*) and, in the event that this is not available, the file lists themselves are regularly maintained in a number of e-mail archive-servers. A partial list of these servers includes:

> *archie@archie.au*
> *archie@archie.doc.ic.ac.uk*
> *archie@archie.mcgill.ca*
> *archie@archie.rutgers.edu*

To use an *archie* server via Telnet, use the response "*archie*" to the prompt "*login:*". No password will be requested. The command *help* will deliver instructions. More information on the use of *archie* is available from *archie-l@cs.mcgill.ca*. The *help* command may also be sent by e-mail to *archive@archie.mcgill.ca*.

Princeton University provides BITNET access to anonymous FTP sites through its mail-server *bitftp@pucc.princeton.edu*. A BITNET-only user sends commands in an e-mail message to "bitftp", which retrieves specified files via FTP and send them on to the user. Users of other networks outside the Internet may avail themselves of the services of Digital Equipment Corp.'s *ftpmail@decurl.dec.com*. In both cases, the command *help* will deliver instructions.

File Access with Usenet and UUCP

UUNET in the US supports a vast number of so-called news groups devoted to the discussion and sharing of information on specific subjects. These news groups, which constitute the Usenet, originated as UNIX user support groups in 1979. Although they serve their own subscribers in the first instance, many items are posted to multiple lists and to outside bulletin boards. The enabling software has been ported to many platforms. The transport methods are based on UUCP, which works by polling [see p. 35], and Network News Transport Protocol (NNTP), which is significantly more flexible. Usenet will often accept addresses in the format used by the Internet.

An archive of Usenet postings and specific addressing information, maintained at the Massachusetts Institute of Technology, is available by FTP from *pit-manager.mit.edu* in the directory */pub/usenet*. Information on Usenet software can be found in *news.admin*. Prospective users should see the contents of *news.announce.newusers*. To retrieve an index of the files of a specific news group, send the message

send index from < comp.sources.misc >

to the address *uunet!netlib*.

File retrieval via UUCP might use a command in the format

uucp -r site!path/to/file

Usenet news groups exist for every major computer platform and many areas of application, so there are dozens of places where one might find discussions relevant to music. Some platform-based groups are:

comp.sources.acorn

comp.sources.amiga

comp.sources.atari.st

comp.sources.mac

comp.sources.msdos

comp.sources.sun

comp.sources.unix

A similar series of groups resides under the heading *comp.sys.* and ends with the extension *.misc*; increasingly there are groups devoted to highly specific topics. The group *comp.sys.ibm.pc.soundcard*, for example, was organized in July 1992. [It is moderated by Christian Vandendorpe: *vandendo@qucis.queensu.ca*.] The *Sound Site Newsletter* (1990—) moderated by David Konatsu (*sound@ccb.ucsf.edu*) is published quarterly on *comp.sys.ibm.pc.misc* and *rec.games.misc*. These examples give only the narrowest glimpse of the activities conducted by news groups. Queries and comments about music software appear sporadically in many Usenet discussions, which are collectively archived in *ftp.uu.net*. Of special note is a news list for network specialists: *info-nets@think.com*.

Further Resources

Internet Resource Guides

Further information on the Internet may be obtained by sending a message to *resource-guide-request@nnsc.nsf.net* or via FTP from *nnsc.nsf.net*: */resource-guide*. An Internet mailing guide is available by FTP from *ra.msstate.edu*: */pub/docs*. Currently available mailing lists can be identified in the file *interest-groups* in the directory */netinfo* at the site *ftp.nisc.sri.com*.

Lists of Lists

The number of list servers, digests, and electronic conferences now in existence is ever-larger and constantly in flux. Diane Kovacks (*librk329@ksuvxa.kent.edu*) has assembled a directory of academic conferences in the humanities and social sciences. These are distributed in three files available by FTP: *acadlist.file1*, *acadlist.file2*, and *acadlist.file3*. She also provides an explanatory document named *acadlist.readme*. Alternatively, a hardcopy version is available for $20US plus $5 postage from the Office of Scientific and Academic Computing, Association of Research Libraries, 1527 New Hampshire Avenue NW, Washington, DC 20036; fax (202) 462-7849.

Shareware, Freeware, and Public Domain Software

Approximately 70,000 users consult the listings of files held in the FTP archives at Vaasa, Finland (*garbo.uwasa.fi*), because numerous utility programs for MS DOS (2,800+ items) and *Windows* reside in them. More than 1,000,000 programs have been downloaded from this facility. See *pc/INDEX.ZIP*. Prospective contributors may write to the moderator, Timo Salmi, (Faculty of Accounting and Industrial Management, University of Vaasa, SF-65101, Finland) at *ts@uwasa.fi* or *salmi@finfun*. The *IP* address is 128.214.87.1.

Address Directories

There are no directories of all individual users connected to a host, but a database of host listings for BITNET, UUCP, and the Internet is made available by Merit, Inc. Access is by *Telnet* to *hermes.merit.edu* (respond to the prompt with the word "*netmailsites*"). Within a specified domain (*e.g.*, *galaxy.edu*), the *whois* database yields the full name and address of users registered with the Network Information Center (*nic.ddn.mil*). The BITEARN nodes list accessible on many academic mainframes can be accessed on VM machines by typing "*Bitnodes*".

Host/User Registration

Those interested in establishing an Internet domain may download a form by FTP from *netinfo/domain-template.txt* on the host *NIC.DDN.MIL*. The same host provides an application form for obtaining an Internet IP number [*netinfo/internet-number-template.txt*] and for user registration [*netinfo/user-template.text*]. These forms should be returned to the *HOSTMASTER@NIC.DDN.MIL*. The services are also provided by mail to DDN Network Information Center, 14200 Park Meadow Drive, Ste. 200, Chantilly, VA 22021; tel. (800) 365-3642. BITNET and UUCP sites can register domain names with the Internet by retrieving forms respectively from *netserv@bitnic* and *uunet!postmaster*.

An FTP Cornucopia:
Miscellaneous archives of possible interest to musicologists

Network tools and documentation:

Appletalk package	*network.ucsd.edu*
info-zip; zip/unzip source	*valeria.cs.ucla.edu*
NNTP	*sunic.sunet.se*
TCP/IP files	*risc.ua.edu*
Telnet, Sendmail	*umaxc.weeg.uiowa.edu*
Telnet (Mac)	*splicer.cba.hawaii.edu*
Usenet archive "news.announce.newsgroups"	*turbo.bio.net*

System tools and documentation:

Atari ST software	*mail-server@cs.ruu.nl*
IBM anti-viral files	*risc.ua.edu*
IBM drivers for TCP/IP	*vm.utdallas.edu*
Macintosh archives	*sumex-aim.stanford.edu*
Macintosh archives	*mac.archive.umich.edu*
Macintosh software (sites for)	*info.umd.edu: ftpsites/mac*
MS DOS archive	*um.cc.umich.edu*
MS DOS public domain software	*nz20.rz.uni-karlsruhe.de*
PC software archives	*mailserv@garbo.uwasa.fi*

Fonts/Printing aids:

Music fonts	*sumex-aim.stanford.edu*
MuTeX	*relay.cdunet.ca*
MuTeX	*ftp.gmd.de: music/musictex and /mutex*
MusicTeX.tar (UNIX)	*mail-server@cs.ruu.nl*
MusicTeX.zip (DOS)	*mail-server@cs.ruu.nl*

Music Printing/Documentation:

Common Music Notation [program]	*ccrma-ftp.stanford.edu: pub/cmn.tar.Z*
Lime: demo copy via Internet	e-mail to: *L-Haken@uiuc.edu*
Nutation [object-oriented notation]	*ccrma-ftp.stanford.edu: pub*
Ph.D. thesis [G. Diener] on *Nutation*	*ccrma-ftp.stanford.edu: pub*

Sound Applications/Documentation:

Z-[MIDI] *Sequencer* [for the NeXT]	*cs.orst.edu: pub/next/binaries*
MIDI; sound bites for SPARCstation	*ucsd.edu*

NeXTrt [sound-file mixer for the NeXT]   *princeton.edu: pub/music*
SPASM [vocal tract simulation]   *ccrma-ftp.stanford.edu: pub*
Ph.D. thesis [P. Cook] on *SPASM*   *ccrma-ftp.stanford.edu: pub*

Journal Archives and Bibliographies:
  discographies   *vacs.uwp.wisc.edu*
  Ethnomusicology Research Digest   *info.umd.edu*
  Music-Research-Digest archives [outside UK] *cattell.psych.upenn.edu*
  Music-Research-Digest archives [UK]   *comlab.oc.ac.uk*

Additional References

Hunt, Craig. *TCP/IP Network Administration*. Sebastopol, CA: O'Reilly and Associates, Inc., 1992.

Kehoe, Brendan. *Zen and the Art of the Internet: A Beginner's Guide*. Englewood Cliffs, NJ: Prentice Hall, 1993. [Earlier versions are available online.]

Thomas, Eric. *LISTSERV Database Functions*, rec. edn. Paris: Ecole Normale Superiore, 1988. [Published online only. Friendly to musicians, as many of the examples are taken from a discographic database of opera materials.].

Credits

This commentary has been written primarily by Eleanor Selfridge-Field with valuable contributions from Walter B. Hewlett, Tom Mathiesen, and Lee Rothfarb, and general advice and other assistance from Philip Baczewski, Louis Bookbinder, Annelies Hoogscarspel, Bill Schottstaedt, and Karl Signell.

Forum on Networking Issues:

Scholarly Communication in the Network Environment

Automatic access to electronic archives and anonymous retrieval of stored files raise challenging issues of identification, ownership, and management of information. These issues are briefly explored in the invited statements of the *Forum* section that follows. Readers are welcome to reply.

The immediacy of the questions raised is so pervasive throughout the academic world that a special enquiry into "information infrastructure" is being conducted in 1992-93. A draft background paper outlining issues, "Scholarly Communication in the Network Environment," is available by e-mail and FTP. This one-year project currently consists of six computer conferences concerned with the following topics and questions:

(1) **Joint authorship and ownership**: How should jointly authored research be structured and how should publication processes be handled?

(2) **Rights in computer conferencing**: What are reasonable expectations for the handling and reuse of messages and other material posted to groups and mailing lists?

(3) **Derivative and iterative works**: What practices should apply to sequenced and variant publications of the same and related works?

(4) **Control of dissemination**: To what extent should key scholarly resources be controlled by particular scholars or organizations?

(5) **Site licensing**: How will widespread site licensing affect access to information by unaffiliated individuals and small firms and organizations?

(6) **International access**: How should researchers and practitioners in the developing world be assured access to research results?

It is intended that a live conference in Washington, DC, early in 1993 will lead to the establishment of policy guidelines.

Brian Kahin, the project director, may be reached at the Science, Technology and Public Policy Program, John F. Kennedy School of Government, Harvard University, 79 John F. Kennedy St., Cambridge, MA 02138; tel. (617) 495-8903; fax (617) 495-5776; e-mail: *kahin@hulaw1. harvard.edu*. **Paul Peters**, the director of the Coalition for Networked Information, may be reached at 1527 New Hampshire Ave., NW, Washington, DC 20036; tel. (202) 232-2466; fax

(202) 462-7849; e-mail: *paul@cni.org*. To request the background paper use FTP to *ftp.cni.org*, login as *anonymous*, use your e-mail address as a password, change directory to */CNI/projects/Harvard.scp*, and get the file *background.txt*.

Online archives must face resolution of the issues described in this draft document every day. In its online *Ethnomusicology Research Digest*, the *EthnoFORUM* service, moderated and maintained by Karl Signell, has crafted a number of well-considered statements about the value of electronic communications. We quote with permission the following one from Issue 30 (20 December 1990):

Electronic Publication as Scholarly Communication

"We have created an expensive machine that suppresses the life force of our society."

The Society for Ethnomusicology spends two-thirds of its budget on printing and mailing the journal [*Ethnomusicology*] and newsletter. Submissions to the journal have been alarmingly low for years, and response to its content is virtually nil. Members who can afford ... [the expense] attend a three-day annual meeting. At most sessions, time for response to a paper is severely limited except when the paper runs overtime and there is no time at all. Inadvertently, we have created an expensive machine which suppresses the life force of our mission: scholarly discussion.

"Electronic publication encourages discussion."

Electronic publication encourages discussion. Printing and mailing expenses are virtually zero. *EthnoFORUM* cannot remotely claim to replace the journal, newsletter, or annual meeting, but it is the first step towards forging a new ethnomusicology community, more vital and more closeknit than before, serving our far-flung readers, researchers, students, and librarians.

ERD has also debated rights of reuse and citation of its material and has adopted the following positions:

Copyright statement:

Authors retain copyright but allow *EthnoFORUM* to publish, distribute, and archive the text electronically. After it has appeared in *EthnoFORUM*, the paper may be republished in any form the author wishes, electronically or in a paper journal, on the condition that the original locus and full citation information for the *EthnoFORUM* version is clearly indicated in any re-publication.

Citation example:

Bel, Bernard. 1991. "Equipentatonic tuning," *Ethnomusicology Research Digest* 38 (18 March), lines 57-114. Electronic file retrievable by anonymous FTP or Telnet as ERD 38 (ERD 91-038) from *INFO. UMD. EDU* (128.8.10.29), directory *ReadingRoom/NewsLetters/ EthnoMusicology/Digest*.

The *TML* has investigated relationships between the printed and electronic word from a different perspective. It is in a different position from *ERD*, since it reuses preexisting material. This position paper clarifying the relationship between versions was written by Tom Mathiesen especially for *CM*:

Copyright Issues in Electronic Communication

The past few years have seen a rapid development of electronic discussion lists (moderated or not), computerized databases on CD-ROM, and true online databases run by private commercial firms, universities, and government agencies. More recently, online journals, such as the *Bryn Mawr Classical Review*, have begun to appear, available to subscribers simply for the cost of logging on to a local mainframe and capturing the data as it comes into their electronic mailboxes.

"Electronic text ...is essentially fluid in nature."

Unlike traditional print media, electronic text can be nearly instantaneously and simultaneously transmitted all over the world, its use cannot be easily monitored by traditional market standards, and because it is not distributed in a fixed medium, it is essentially fluid in nature.

These characteristics raise a number of issues pertaining to copyright, some of which are beginning to be explored by the Information Infrastructure Project in the Science, Technology, and Public Policy Program at Harvard University's John F. Kennedy School of Government.[1]

The *Thesaurus Musicarum Latinarum* (*TML*), an online database of Latin music theory (see reports in *CM 1990*, p. 133; *CM 1991*, pp. 37-39), anticipated two copyright issues when it began to be conceived in 1989. Both of these are traditional copyright questions, but they take on new meaning in the current environment of broadly accessible electronic databases.

"Does conversion of printed texts into electronic form violate copyright?"

The first question was: Would it be a violation of copyright to convert printed texts into electronic form and place them on publicly accessible mainframe systems of distribution, from which they could be retrieved by any subscriber to the system?

The second was: Could the *TML* claim copyright on the structure and design of its system and its particular compilation of electronic texts?

The *TML* was certainly not the first project to undertake the conversion of large quantities of printed text into electronic form. In general, earlier text database projects seem to have taken the position that conversion of printed data into an electronic form licensed to individual users or sites exclusively for the purpose of scholarly study would be permitted under the law. In order to insure this very narrow and limited use, the electronic media produced by these projects were not sold and could only be obtained under a restrictive license.

"The TML wanted to make its resources available to as many scholars as possible."

The *TML*, by contrast, wanted to make its resources as broadly and easily available to as many scholars as possible, and it therefore took the position that texts under copyright could only be used with the permission of the publisher.

Moreover, the *TML* never regarded its database as in any sense a substitute for the "original" printed or manuscript forms; the TML's texts are, rather, complementary versions that allow computers to undertake and greatly accelerate at least two traditionally laborious tasks of textual criticism: (1) searching texts for words, text strings, or various combinations controlled by Boolean operators; and (2) comparing different versions of texts to locate changes, deletions, replacements, and moves. When a user discovers points of interest within texts by employing the *TML*, it directs the user to those points within the original form, which remains the principal object of study. Perhaps because copyright holders recognized that the *TML* represents an enhancement of traditional media rather than a threat to their interests, they have, with a single exception, been willing to have their texts placed on the *TML* without the need for any cumbersome or restrictive licensing.

As to the second question, the *TML* believes that it clearly owns the rights to its name, the structure and design of its system, and the actual compilation of texts, each individual text of which is in the public domain or under separate copyright. Although it is conceivable that some entity might copy the entire *TML* with the idea of making it available through some system other than Indiana University's mainframes, it is difficult to imagine any incentive to do so.

As it stands, the *TML* is available to subscribers all over the world free of charge, it is continuously maintained by the Project Director and the Project and Editorial Committees, and it is to the *TML* that copyright holders have granted permission for the use of their texts. Thus, there could be no commercial incentives to copy the *TML* or any of its parts, and a facsimile of the *TML* would have neither permission from copyright holders to use their texts nor the key personnel who operate the system—a matter of some im-

"Electronic and print media should be viewed as complementary extensions of one another."

portance, since online databases, unlike print media, do require continuing personnel support.

The draft document of the Information Infrastructure Project raises some very important questions about the uncertain application of copyright law to various forms of electronic distribution. It is, however, important to keep in mind that electronic media and traditional print media are fundamentally different forms. If conceived as competing media, the copyright issues will naturally drive them apart.

In my opinion, electronic and print media should be viewed as complementary extensions of one another, each with its own advantages and disadvantages. In this view, copyright holders and database developers can work together to their mutual advantage and the advantage of scholarship. For its part, copyright law can recognize legitimate claims to right of content without unduly hampering natural and beneficial extensions of media.

—Thomas J. Mathiesen

[1] See Brian Kahin, "Scholarly Communication in the Network Environment: Issues of Principle, Policy, and Practice," distributed electronically from *Kahin@hulaw1.harvard.edu* [and as described on p. 55].

Contact information for **Thomas J. Mathiesen**, project director of the *Thesaurus Musicarum Latinarum*, and for **Karl Signell**, director of the *EthnoFORUM*, is given on p. 44.

Musical Information

Max Haas:

Chatull Gadol 1.0

Chatull Gadol ["Big Cat" in Yiddish] is a program, running on the Macintosh under *HyperCard*, for the study and comparison of medieval monophonic repertories. Its primary purpose is to introduce research students to the kinds of musicological problems that pertain to these repertories and to offer a prototype that could be refined or adapted to the specific needs of one repertory or time-frame. It represents an effort to adapt the computer science concept of "rapid prototyping" to a specific problem typology in musicology.

The software comes with a database of several hundred liturgical chants. These include Gregorian settings of the Introit, Gradual, Alleluia, Tract, Offertory, and Communion and their equivalents in Old Roman chant, as well as examples from the Beneventan and Ambrosian rites. Textual items of information about each work include the incipit, mode, chant family, liturgical function, and source. The "gamut" of stored pitches stretches from *E* to *b'*.

Searches of both variant settings of a common text and of specific melodic strings are facilitated. In the retrieval of multiple chants on a common text, alignment is by text syllable. In searches for specific pitch sequences, a number of Boolean constraints can be implemented. Transpositions and inversions can be recognized. Search results can be displayed on the screen or presented in statistical charts and in bar graphs created from them. A *play* command is also supported.

The program supports the simultaneous display of up to four versions and provides some predefined functions for pattern matching. It is a non-commercial program with screen prompts in English and an extensive manual in German. While the author claims it as his intellectual property, he explicitly authorizes users to make modifications and copies. Those wishing to use the database independently of the program will need a copy of the commercial database software *Omnis5*.

References

Mullin, Mark. *Rapid Prototyping for Object-Oriented Systems*. Reading, MA: Addison-Wesley, 1990.

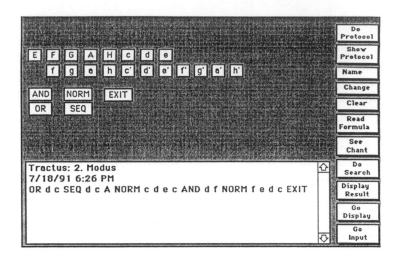

Chatull Gadol: Screen menu for construction of search expressions.

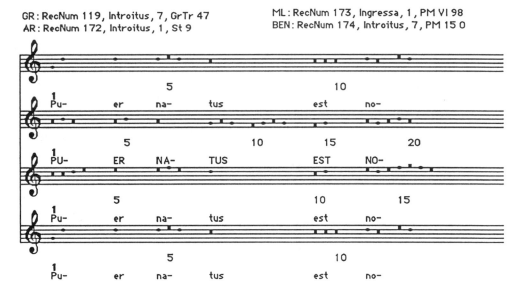

GR: RecNum 119, Introitus, 7, GrTr 47   ML: RecNum 173, Ingressa, 1, PM VI 98
AR: RecNum 172, Introitus, 1, St 9   BEN: RecNum 174, Introitus, 7, PM 15 0

Chatull Gadol: Vertical alignment of corresponding text syllables
in four settings of the introit for Christmas.

Max Haas is a member of the academic staff of Basel University. Chatull Gadol has been developed in his spare time. The program, documentation, and data are available for the cost of copying and postage [the equivalent of roughly $15US]. Enquiries and orders may be addressed to him at Leimenweg 10, CH-4419 Lupsingen, Switzerland.

John Stinson:

The *SCRIBE* Database

The *SCRIBE* database of fourteenth-century music and related repertories has been developed and maintained at La Trobe University, Australia, for five years. It now contains 4,408 fully-encoded works. Analytical tools have recently been developed for melodic analysis. These have enabled researchers to test some of the established theories about the behavior of modal music and to quantify many of the generalizations made about different chant repertories.

The Dominican chant has the advantage of having been "reformed" according to well-formulated rules in the mid-thirteenth century, and of having much new repertoire written in the fourteenth century (277 works). In addition, 105 Cypriot chants have been compared to the other Dominican compositions and both repertories to the older body of chant. Some hypotheses about the composition of late medieval chant can now be proposed. These will be put forth in the published versions of papers given in Cyprus and Madrid in April 1992.

Efforts to encode these repertories have raised certain questions about music written before the end of the sixteenth century. These relate especially to the ubiquity of chant, both in its own right and as the basis for polyphonic compositions; to the necessity of accommodating various systems of notation involving staff lines numbering from none to six; and to a variety of rhythmic interpretations of the same note-shapes.

In related developments, Ruth Steiner (Catholic University, Washington, DC) has made available for cross-referencing four large files of text information about particular chant repertories and an index of over 14,000 chant items. Because none of these have any music, a package of 4,564 chant melodies is being prepared in various forms which can be linked to her databases to provide the missing tunes. These will be in *dBASE* format. The melodies are in letter notation and three kinds of interval notation (related to the first note, the *finalis*, and the immediately preceding note), which are useful for some kinds of research but do not represent the notation as completely as is done in *SCRIBE*.

John Stinson *is in the Department of Music, La Trobe University, Bundoora, Victoria 3083, Australia; tel. +61 03-479-2879; fax +61 03-478-5814; e-mail: MUSJS@lure.latrobe.edu.au.*
SCRIBE *has been described in previous articles in CM, including "Encoding Neumes and Mensural Notation" (1990, pp. 25ff).*

Helmut Schaffrath:

The *ESAC* Databases and *MAPPET* Software

The *MAPPET* [Music Analysis Package for Ethnomusicology] programs and their associated databases of monophonic music continue to increase. There are now well over 10,000 melodies encoded ASCII and stored in Essen; more than 8000 of these are available without charge by license. Notational capabilities provided by the *ESTAFF* program have been expanded over the past year. A new program called *SAMMY* converts analytical data from the *ANA*[lysis] program into a database format for the Atari. *MAPPET* software runs on PCs and provides support for users who wish to encode their own data. An increasing number of users have taken advantage of this capability [see, for example, the following report by Lelio Camilleri].

When storing *ESAC* (either by typing or by running the *MIDI* input program), the first step is to define phrases. To accomplish this, each phrase is encoded on a separate line in one field of a relational (*AskSam*) database. In vocal music there is usually no ambiguity about phrase definition: one looks immediately at a phrase-delineated melody and understands the structure of the melody. [In some recent examples, including that shown in *CM 1991* on p. 31, the line-based representation of phrases, always starting with a pickup, was altered to facilitate correspondence with notated examples, always ending with a barline.]

Any formal analysis by the program *ANA* reflects this structure. So when one reads, for instance, that the pitch form is a-b-a-b, one can compare this directly with lines 1-2-3-4. The translation program now reproduces this internal representation perfectly and can display the analytical results to the right of each staff when the user requests it. A three-page printout demonstrating eleven different ways of representing one melody line encoded in *ESAC*, just by pressing the right button, has been created.

----

*The **ESAC** files and **MAPPET** software and documentation are available by license from the developer, **Helmut Schaffrath**. They are free of cost to scholars. To obtain a license agreement, contact Prof. Dr. Schaffrath at the Universität Essen, FB 4 - Musik - Postfach, W-4300 Essen 1, Germany; e-mail: JMP100@DE0HRZ1A.BITNET. Atari users who are interested in **SAMMY** software may contact **Christoph Dammann**, Fleischhauerstr. 34, D-2400 Lübeck 1, Germany.*

Lelio Camilleri:

The *Lieder* of Karl Collan

The Finnish composer Karl Collan (1828-1873) was recognized as a distinguished composer and collector of *Lieder*. The melodies of the 21 *Lieder* in Collan's first book (1847) have been encoded in *ESAC* code using *MAPPET* software [see the preceding report]. This repertory was chosen because of its homogeneous nature and stylistic regularity for the exploration of different methodologies.

Two different kinds of analytical approaches have been attempted. First, all the procedures supported by Helmut Schaffrath's software have been tried. These include analytical investigations of mode, contour, pitch patterns, rhythmic patterns, and other musical features, all carried out using *MAPPET* software. The results have been displayed and subsequently investigated by means of *ESTAFF* facilities.

Second, the program for paradigmatic analysis, based on semiotic theory, that was previously developed at our facility [*CM 1990*, p. 119] has been employed. The *Lieder* melodies have been searched for signifying units (Ruwet, 1972; Camilleri *et al.*, forthcoming). [A signifying unit is the longest unit used at least twice in a work. Units acquire significance within a network of structural relationships.] Derivations have also been found. One of the relevant findings is that these melodies use minimal units as generators of the main melodic figures. The analytical searches made by *MAPPET* permit indexing of the pitches used in each melody and consideration of these in relation to the melodic contour.

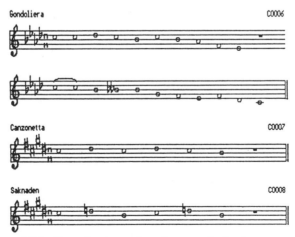

Melodic reductions, based on semiotic theory,
of Collan's *Lieder* "Gondoliera," "Canzonetta," and "Saknaden."

In a further phase, the second book of *Lieder* will also be encoded and further analytical searches on the entire corpus will be carried out.

References

Camilleri, Lelio. "Paradigmatic Analysis with the Computer" in the *Proceedings of the Second European Conference on Music Analysis*, ed. Rossana Dalmonte and Mario Baroni. Trent: University Press, forthcoming.

Ruwet, Nicolas. *Musique, language, poesie*. Paris: Du Seuil, 1972.

Schaffrath, Helmut. "The Retrieval of Monophonic Melodies and their Variants: Concepts and Strategies in Computer-Aided Analysis" in *Computer Models and Representations of Music*, ed. Alan Marsden and Anthony Pople. London: Academic Press, 1992.

Lelio Camilleri is at the Conservatorio di Musica «L. Cherubini», Divisione Musicologica CNUCE-C.N.R., Piazza delle Belle Arti 2, 50122 Firenze, Italy; tel. +39 55-282105; fax. +39 55-2396785; e-mail: CONSERVA@IFIIDG.FI.CNR.IT.

J. Marshall Bevil:

MelAnaly

MelAnaly is a body of genre- and task-specific software for the comparative analysis of British and British-American folk tunes, specifically the archetypal, dual-strain tunes that are governed by a corpus of morphological norms and the tonal constraints of the anhemitonic gamut (Bevil 1985, 1986, and 1991).

Comparison involves two steps, the first of which is a computer-assisted scan of arrays that contain numeric codes for the pitch, duration, and stress factors of specified control and test variants. The second step is the application of seventeen sets of programmed parameters defining the various natures and extents of melodic kinships. Results of the array scan are printed in a table and a set of melodic contour graphs (Hewlett and Selfridge-Field, pp. 115 and 119).

MelAnaly, in its present form, is of limited applicability to genres not possessing the stylistic traits of the Insular ballad or fiddle melody. However, the analytical principle of equal emphasis on main motifs and overall contour at a multiplicity of strata is adaptable to other species through alteration of array sizes and other modifications. Repertories within which harmonic criteria are of critical significance can be addressed through the addition of one or more array dimensions.

The software package is designed for the Apple IIGS with a minimum of 256 RAM and a resident cache for permanent file and temporary program storage. Data input during file preparation is achieved through single keystrokes that are automatically converted to numeric codes developed by the author.

Limited availability of the database, via modem, on a subscription basis, is projected for 1994, and the availability of the complete software package to remote operators is projected by or before 2000. Accessibility will be via both conventional and wireless modem.

References

Bevil, J. Marshall. "Centonization and Concordance in the American Southern Uplands Folksong Melody: A Study of the Musical Generative and Transmittive Processes of an Oral Tradition," Ph.D. dissertation, University of North Texas, 1984. Available on microfiche from UNT and on microfilm from University Microfilms International, Ann Arbor, MI.

Bevil, J. Marshall. "Scale in Southern Appalachian Folksong: A Reexamination," *College Music Symposium*, 26 (1986), 77-91.

Bevil, J. Marshall. "The Ongoing Development of the *MelAnaly* Software Package for the Comparative Analysis of British and British-American Folk Tunes," read at the Second International Conference on Computers in Music Research, Queen's University of Belfast, 1991. Copies of handout and companion videotape available on request.

Hewlett, Walter B., and Eleanor Selfridge-Field (eds.). *Directory of Computer-Assisted Research in Musicology*, (Menlo Park, California: Center for Computer Assisted Research in the Humanities, 1988).

J. Marshall Bevil can be contacted at 7918 Millbrook Drive, Coppercreek, Wheatstone Village, Houston, TX 77095; tel. (713) 859-5965.

Spyros K. Gardikiotis:

Melody

The aims of the *Melody* computer program are to archive one-part melodies, to classify them by musical and non-musical criteria (style, scale, composer, place), and to create concordances based on objective elements which define to a considerable degree the style of songs of the most widespread kinds of music. These elements are the intervals and the durations of notes.

The comparison of these elements is realized using the linear relation coefficient and the G coincidence factor, a measure that was invented by the author [reported in *CM 1991*, p. 79]. This application is written in the *Clipper* database language and uses a special encoding system. A facility to import and export data in other popular formats is planned.

The database contains 30 songs of light Greek music which have been used to test the program. The long-term objectives of the study are (1) the creation and manipulation of a database of Greek (including Byzantine, folk, etc.) melodies; (2) the investigation of the differences and similarities between melodies of the same or other style; and (3) the creation of a statistical image of the melodies according to their intervals and durations.

In the example on the facing page, linear coefficients of pitch values, of successive pairs of pitches, and of intervallic change are expressed as floating-point numbers and the G-coincidence factor as a percentage. The ambitus is given in cents. [A semitone = 100 cents.] These provide a basis for study of stylistic traits in a given repertory and comparison between repertories.

The *Melody* program manipulates any melody, even if it is not in Western European notation. For example, it can handle Byzantine, Indian, and Arabian melodies. This capability is supported by the use of one-cent steps, user-definable intervals in the melodic encoding, and user-definable micro-durations. The program can also run external (user-definable) programs for input, editing, and output of data. There is no present capability of encoding glissandi or similar effects.

At this time the program messages and the corresponding manuals are in Greek.

References

Gardikiotis, Spyridon K. "Computer program for filing and correlating melodies," Master's Thesis, Aristotle University of Thessaloniki, 1990.

Καρτέλλα Νο 0 με 11   Σύνολο φθογγοσήμων : 151
Τίτλος της μελωδίας που συγκρίνεται: Μαρία (ΜΟΥΖΑΚΗΣ ΓΙΩΡΓΟΣ)

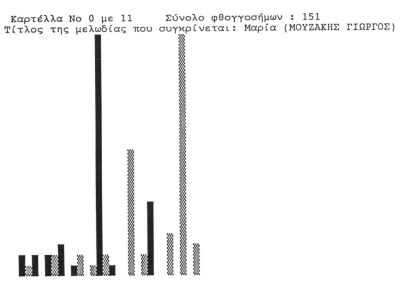

| Καρτέλλα | 11 | / | Πέρσι τέτοιο καιρό |

Συσχέτιση αξιών

Συντελεστής συσχέτισης :   -0.195408956
Πιθανά λάθη   :
Σύμπτωση G : 8%

Συσχέτιση αξιών ανα ζεύγος

Συντελεστής συσχέτισης :   -0.102495046
Πιθανά λάθη   :
Σύμπτωση G : 6%

. . . .
Συσχέτιση διαστημάτων

Ambitus : Δεν υπάρχει το διάστημα στο αρχείο διαστημάτων   1500 cent(s)

Συντελεστής συσχέτισης :   0.767082664
Πιθανά λάθη   :
Σύμπτωση G : 73%

Statistical output from the program *Melody*.

The bar graph shows the distribution of frequencies of intervals and durations in the song "Marìa," containing 151 events, by Mouzakis George. Three measures of correlation are employed.

Spyros [Spiridon] Gardikiotis can be reached at Raidestou 45, 171 22 N. Smirni, Athens, Greece; tel. +30 1/9300461, 1/7780777. He hopes to continue this project in another setting and eventually to provide an English-language version of the program and its documentation.

John Morehen:

The Speech-Melodies of Leoš Janáček

During the last thirty years of his life the Czech composer Leoš Janáček collected examples of casual speech in conventional musical notation, in much the same way as Olivier Messiaen notated bird-song. Several hundred of these short "speech-melodies" have survived in Janáček's notebooks.

Although most are syllabic settings and merely incorporate the natural speech inflections of just one or two words, others involve longer melodic phrases of perhaps a dozen or more notes. This study of Janáček's approach to the composition of these speech-melodies is expected to throw light on his attitude to composition in general.

The analytical programs are written in *SNOBOL4/SPITBOL* and the data is encoded in *DARMS76.*

John Morehen *is Professor of Music, the University of Nottingham, University Park, Nottingham NG7 2RD, UK; +44 0602/515151; fax +44 0602/420825; e-mail AMZJM@VAX.NOTTINGHAM. AC.UK.* **Matthew Holmes** *and* **John Tyrrell** *are also participating in this research project.*

F. E. Ann Osborn-Seyffert:

Analysis and Classification of Singing Games

In considering the adaptation of the instructional programs of Zoltán Kodály for use in Canadian schools, the musical characteristics of Canadian children's songs had to be differentiated from and substituted for those of Hungarian songs. In a preliminary study, the historical relationships of the singing games were examined, then variants were transcribed to a common G final and analyzed manually. In a subsequent dissertation (Osborn, 1986), a computer-aided methodology was developed to analyze the tones of the phrases of the singing games to discover their characteristic phrase patterns. This approach was different from earlier analytical studies that had attempted to summarize the most frequently occurring characteristics and to find common ground for comparison between music of all times and places. *MUSICODE-A* (Blombach, 1976) was adapted to encode four parameters of single-voice melodies: the letter name, accidental, octave register, and duration. The programs were written in *SNOBOL-4*.

The major problem of the analysis program was to compare phrases of variants in different time signatures. It had been observed in the preliminary study that, between variants, the main and secondary stressed beats of each meter contained the structurally more important melodic information. Thus, the coded pitch information of each phrase was reduced to an eighth note value for each measure of 2/4, 3/4, and 6/8 meters and to a quarter note value for each measure of 4/4 meter. Separate program statements for each time signature were required to extract the reduced coded pitches of main, secondary, and unstressed beats. A three-dimensional array was created to tabulate the phrase number (X), the processed variant row number (Y), and the column number (Z), which included the variant identification number, time signature, anacrusis (if present), and all stress-/unstressed-beat reduced coded pitches. The reduced coded pitches were then extracted from main and secondary stressed beat columns for each phrase. The resulting pattern of each phrase was compared with all others and printed out only once, with sources listed as "X,Y". The output for first-phrase patterns is represented below.

Coded Pitch Patterns (Z)	Phrase Position and Processed Variant Number (X,Y)
GN4 BN3 GN4 GN4	1,1;
GN4 GN4 GN4 GN4	1,2;1,3;1,4;4,12;
GN4 GN4 DN5 GN4	1,5;1,19;3,5;3,19;
CN5 BN4 AN4 DN4	1,6;1,7;1,8;3,6;3,7;3,8;
DN5 DN5 DN5 DN5	1,9;1,10;1,11;3,4;3,9;3,10;3,11;
B-4 B-4 B-4 B-4	1,12;
DN4 GN4 EN4 DN4	1,13;
DN5 DN5 BN4 DN5	1,14;1,15;1,16;1,17;1,18;3,14;3,15;3,16;3,17;3,18;
GN4 AN4 CN5 AN4	1,20;1,21;1,22;1,23;3,20;2,21;3,22,3,23;
DN4 F#4 AN4 GN4	1,24;3,24;
GN4 BN4 DN5	1,25;3,25;
GN4 BN4 DN5 BN4	1,26;1,36;3,26;3,36;
DN5 DN5 BN4 GN4	1,27;1,28;3,27;3,28;4,6;4,8;
DN5 BN4 CN5 AN4	1,29;3,29;
B-4 B-4 CN5 AN4	1,30;1,31;1,32;1,33;1,34;3,30;3,31,3;32,3,33,3,34;
GN4 GN4 DN5 DN5	1,35;1,36;

Coded pitch patterns and their phrase position in the variant.

Since that study (summarized in Osborn, 1988) was completed, all variants have been encoded. These can now be analyzed for their phrase patterns, regardless of the number of sections and phrases. For each of the groupings analyzed according to the number of phrases, successive programs will analyze the cadence tones and then the range of each variant. Only six texts in the collection are isometric. The final results should reveal the common musical characteristics of this collection of singing games.

The initial application of the results is foreseen to be in the development of a more effective approach to musical literacy programs for young children. Researchers and educators in other countries could adapt the encoding and analysis programs to their song literature for both comparative and educational purposes. It is to be expected that for a particular linguistic culture the musical characteristics will be unique. It is hoped that comparisons with adult folksong repertories can later be made.

References

Blombach, Ann K. "A Conceptual Framework for the Use of the Computer in Musical Analysis." Ph.D. Dissertation, The Ohio State University, 1976.

Osborn, F. E. Ann. "A Computer-aided Methodology for the Analysis and Classification of British-Canadian Children's Traditional Singing Games," Ph.D. Dissertation, The Ohio State University, 1986.

Osborn, F. E. Ann. "A Computer-aided Methodology for the Analysis and Classification of British Canadian Children's Traditional Singing Games," *Computers and the Humanities*, 22 (1988), 173-182.

F. E. Ann Osborn-Seyffert is in the School of Education, Lakehead University, Thunder Bay, ON P7B 5E1, Canada; tel. (807) 343-8726; fax (807) 344-6807.

Andranik Tangian:

A Binary System for Classification of Rhythmic Patterns

The computer simulation of perception of musical time, rhythm, and tempo is complicated by the lack of clear definitions of these concepts. Rhythmic patterns are defined in relation to a certain tempo, whereas tempo is defined in relation to certain rhythmic patterns and time. A possible way to break the circular relationship between these definitions is to consider them from the standpoint of the principle of correlativity of perception (Tangian 1989; 1990).

By the correlativity of perception we mean to identify similar configurations of stimuli and to make them configurations of a higher level. This is equivalent to the description of information in terms of generative elements and their transformations.

In our definition of time, rhythm and tempo are based on the representation of a series of time events in terms of generative elements, *i.e.*, rhythmic patterns repeated with variations and distortions. We consider repeated rhythmic patterns as recognizable determinants of the perception of time.

The possibility of ambiguity in rhythmic segmentation under tempo deviations is overcome by a model of optimal representation of a series of time events. We cannot, however, eliminate all kinds of ambiguity in rhythmic segmentation. The goal of the work described here is to develop an efficient technique for finding and classifying rhythmic patterns which could subsequently be used in a general model of time/rhythm recognition and tempo tracking.

Separation of Rhythmic Patterns

A sequence of identical eighth notes gives an example of periodicity but not of rhythm. To become a rhythm this sequence of durations must be segmented, for example into triplets. However, if we consider the regularity of triplets as indecomposable objects, we are left with periodicity again. Rhythm implies both periodicity and structure.

Periodicity implies that the starting point of the period can be chosen arbitrarily. This is true for infinite sequences but not for a few repetitions, where the choice of the starting point can be essential for the simplest representation of the given sequence of events.

To perceive a rhythm unambiguously, some events must be accentuated to indicate the segmentation. All known ways of accentuation are based on a break in homogeneity and are caused by changes in pitch, harmony, dynamics, timbre, etc. Simplifying the principles of rhythmic segmentation developed by Boroda (1985), we introduce the following rules of rhythmic accentuation.

Rule 1. The only characteristic of a time event is defined to be the duration of time interval between its onset and the onset of the next time event. This inter-onset time interval is called the duration, associated with the event. If the given time event is the last in the sequence, the associated duration is assumed to be of arbitrary length.

Rule 2. To distinguish accentuated events in a sequence of time events at least two types of durations are needed.

Rule 3. A duration associated with an event is said to be accentuated if it is (a) the maximal duration in its neighborhood (*i.e.*, it is longer than the preceding and succeeding one) and (b) the last among similar longer durations (*i.e.*, it is preceded by the same duration, and is succeeded by a shorter one). A duration associated with an event is said to be locally accentuated if it is (c) the first among similar longer ones and is not close to an accentuated event (*i.e.*, it is preceded by a shorter duration and succeeded by the same one, which is not accentuated).

Classification of Rhythmic Patterns

To recognize rhythmic segmentation, we also need information about factors other than accentuation. By rhythmic patterns we mean all possible segments of the given sequence of durations.

Rule 4. A regular rhythmic pattern, or rhythmic phrase, is defined to be a sequence of durations beginning just after an accentuated duration and ending at the accentuated duration. A regular rhythmic pattern with only one accentuated duration is called a rhythmic syllable (Katuar 1926).

The rhythmic syllable is the simplest regular rhythmic pattern. The rhythmic phrase can be regarded as being composed of successive rhythmic syllables. We assume that rhythmic syllables are perceived as indecomposable time units.

Rule 5. An elaboration of a rhythmic pattern is another rhythmic pattern, preserving the pulse, or simply a subdivision of durations of the given pattern by means of insertion of additional time events (Mont-Reynaud and Goldstein 1985).

Figure 1 illustrates the idea of rhythmic elaboration with an example of subdivisions of a single half-note pattern within the accuracy of sixteenths. Each pattern in Figure 1 is supposed to be succeeded by a time event, determining the duration of its last note (otherwise the half-note pattern cannot be defined). The number of unique patterns of the same duration will be used to estimate the complexity of rhythm.

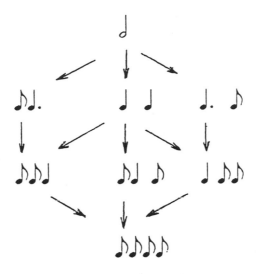

Figure 1.

The idea of elaboration can be explained in terms of the principle of correlativity of perception. In actuality we can represent rhythmic patterns by strings of 0s and 1s. For example, if the smallest desired division of duration is equivalent to a sixteenth note, the top and the bottom patterns in Figure 1 look like {10000000} and {10101010} respectively. It is easy to see that pattern A is the elaboration of pattern B, if and only if A > B, which means that A contains all ones of B. Since the number of ones in B is equal to the autocorrelation $C(B,B)$ of BbB, and the number of coinciding ones in A and B is equal to the correlation $C(A,B)$ of A and B, we derive the result that A is the elaboration of B, if and only if

$$C(A,B) = C(B,B)$$

Since the correlation is usually understood to be a measure of similarity, the reference to the autocorrelation of the pattern, which is supposed to be generative, means that the elaborated pattern must be as similar to the generative one as possible.

Rule 6. The sum of two successive rhythmic patterns is defined to be the rhythmic pattern formed by the time events of these patterns. The fusion of two successive rhythmic syllables is defined to be a rhythmic syllable, which is the elaboration of their sum.

Note that we define the sum of rhythmic patterns for successive ones, since the duration between the two summarized patterns must also be taken into account. The fusion is the result of summation of syllables and transformation of the accentuated event ending the first syllable into a non-accentuated one. For that purpose we shorten the associated duration by means of inserting new time events (*i.e.*, we elaborate the sum of syllables).

Figure 2.

In Figure 2 we give an example of the fusion of two identical rhythmic syllables. The perceived effect is the symmetry of the whole passage, having the structure 1 + 1 + 2. It is easy to see that the duration of the third syllable is the same as the sum of the two syllables. It is an important condition for their fusion. If we change the duration of the first rest, resulting in a change in the duration of the sum of the first two syllables, or if we add notes to the third pattern, we perceive lesser symmetry in the given passage.

The distance between the sum of the two syllables and their fusion is not so important. If we change the duration of the second rest in Figure 2, the third rhythmic syllable is still perceived as the elaboration of the sum of the preceding ones. Here we can draw an analogy with common rhythms, structured like the series 1 + 1 + 2 + 4 + ... The regular recurrence of patterns in such rhythms is only slightly masked by the fusion of rhythmic patterns, and this explains their ease of perception.

Since the number of generative patterns is much less than the number of rhythmic patterns, their classification and grouping is much easier. Therefore the representation of the given sequence of rhythmic patterns in terms of their generative elements reveals internal regularities in rhythm associated with time.

Rule 7. If representation of a given sequence of time events in terms of generative syllables contains repetitions, then the time is determined by ratios between durations of syllables within the repeating group of generative syllables.

With these seven rules we have provided a set of definitions for determining the rhythmic structure of performed music. Now we are going to describe a rhythm by means of rhythmic syllables and then identify their elaborations, sums, and fusions.

A Sample Application

To illustrate the procedure of determining the structure of a simple rhythm, consider the snare drum part from "Bolero" by M. Ravel (Figure 3). We should like to mention that our method uses time data only. It cannot be applied to rhythms defined by pitch contour or dynamical accents.

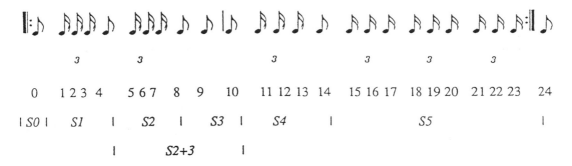

Figure 3.

1. Consider duration 0. It precedes a shorter one and therefore it is accentuated. Since it is the first event in the sequence, we determine syllable SO.

$$SO = \{100\}, \text{ corresponding to } \quad ♪.$$

Now our rhythm is represented as SO.

2. Consider duration 1. It is succeeded by the same duration and therefore it is not accentuated. The same is valid for durations 2 and 3.

3. Duration 4 is accentuated because it succeeds and precedes shorter durations. Consequently, we determine syllable S1, consisting of durations, following SO up to the given durations:

$$S1 = \{111\ 100\}, \text{ corresponding to } \quad ♪♪♪ \ ♪.$$

4. At events 5-7 we have no accentuation and we do not determine syllables.

5. At event 8 we have the same situation as at event 4, with the difference that event 8 is not an accentuated but a locally accentuated event.

        $S2 = \{111\ 100\}$, corresponding to ♪♪♪ ♪.

6. Event 9 is not accentuated.

7. Event 10 is accentuated and we determine syllable S3.

        $S3 = \{100\ 100\}$, corresponding to ♪ ♪.

We find that S1 and S2 are the elaboration of S3 and that S3 is the sum of two syllables SO.

8. Since events 11-13 are not accentuated, we do not determine syllables for them.

9. Event 14 is accentuated and we determine syllable S4.

        $S4 = \{111\ 100\}$, corresponding to ♪♪♪ ♪.

10. Events 15-23 are not accentuated.

11. Event 24 is accentuated and we define syllable S5.

        $S5 = \{111\ 111\ 111\ 100\}$, corresponding to ♪♪♪ ♪♪♪ ♪♪♪ ♪.

Syllable S5 is the elaboration of the sum of syllables $S2 + S3$.

Slightly modifying the assumptions of our analysis, we determine the rhythmic syllabification (phrase, if local accents are not ignored) $S3 + S4$.

        $S3 + 4 = \{111\ 100\ 100\ 100\}$, corresponding to ♪♪♪ ♪ ♪ ♪.

Then rhythmic syllable S6 is the fusion of syllables S3 and S4.

Syllable SO can be interpreted as the end of syllable S5. Finally we find a repeated structure $S1\ S3 + 4$, where $S3 + 4$ is two times longer than S1. This can now be interpreted conventionally as the meter 3/4, 3/8, etc.

References

Boroda, Moisei. "On Some Rules of Rhythmic Recurrence in Folk and Professional Music" [in Gerogian] in *Kompleksnoye Izucheniye Muzykalnogo Tvorchestva: Konzepziya, Problemy, Perspektivy* (Tbilisi: Nauka, 1985), pp. 135-167.

Chafe, Chris, Bernard Mont-Reynaud, and L. Rush. "Toward an Intelligent Editor of Digital Audio: Recognition of Musical Constructs," *Computer Music Journal*, 6/1 (1982), 30-41.

Dannenberg, Roger B., and Bernard Mont-Reynaud. "Following an Improvisation in Real Time," *Proceedings of the 1987 International Computer Music Conference* (San Francisco: Computer Music Association, 1987), pp. 241-248.

Desain, Peter, and Henkjan Honing. "Quantization of Musical Time: A Connectionist Approach," *Computer Music Journal,* 13/3 (1989), 56-66.

Katayose, Haruhiro, and Seiji Inokuchi. "The Kansei Music System," *Computer Music Journal*, 13/4 (1989), 72-77.

Katuar, G. *Ritm (Muzykalnaya Forma, I)*. Moskow, 1926.

Mont-Reynaud, Bernard, and M. Goldstein. "On Finding Rhythmic Patterns in Musical Lines," *Proceedings of the 1985 International Computer Music Conference* (San Francisco: Computer Music Association, 1985), pp. 391-397.

Schloss, W. Andrew. "On the Automatic Transcription of Percussive Music - From Acoustical Signal to High-Level Analysis," Stanford: Stanford University Department of Music Report STAN-M-27, 1985.

Tangian, Andranik. "A Principle of Relativity of Perception and Its Applications to Pattern Recognition in Analysis of Performed Music," *Proceedings of the First International Conference on Music Perception and Cognition, Kyoto, Japan, October 17-19, 1989*, pp. 261-266.

....

*The Armenian composer and musicologist **Andranik Tangian**, formerly of the Soviet Academy of Sciences, is currently engaged in research at A.C.R.O.E., 46, avenue Félix-Viallet, 38000 Grenoble, France; tel. +33 76/57-46-70.*

Ira Braus:

Rhythmic Disambiguation through Computer Modelling

Metrical ambiguity is a common feature of much music from the late nineteenth and early twentieth centuries. In experiments at Bates College, computer-modelled performances are constructed to give accentual readings that conform to the written prescriptions of the score. The programs currently use *CSound* on the NeXT.

One example is provided by Debussy's *Nuages*. While the piece is notated in 6/4 (implying a 3 + 3 subdivision of the measure), it is invariably played as if it were in 3/2 (with 2 + 2 + 2 pairing of beats). Albert Bregman (1990) notes that consecutive fifths and octaves intensify streaming among different timbres. The open fifths occurring in Example 1 on the odd-numbered beats are cases in point. Conventional analysis supports the view that Debussy intended to create suspense by means of metrical ambiguity, which could later be "stabilized."

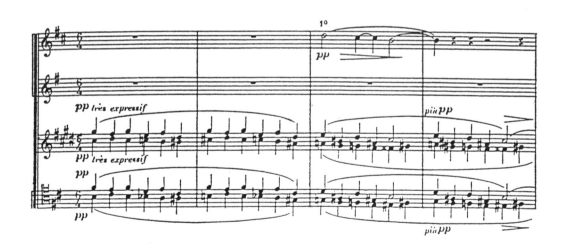

Example 1. Debussy: *Nuages*.

In a computer-modelled performance (using sampled instrumental sounds), the aim is to construct a truly 6/4 reading of *Nuages* by breaking up the fusion of the parallel octaves-with-fifths evoking the 3/2 metrical percept without brute-force accent. In such a performance the macrostructural significance of the Bb (A#) pitch class (beat 4 of each measure in Ex. 1) is emphasized. Its importance is verified in its oscillation with Eb (D#) in the bass of the ensuing passage shown in Example 2.

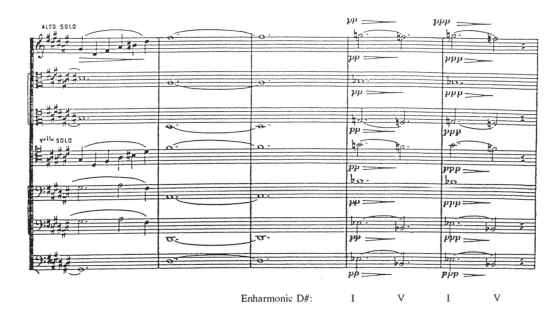

Enharmonic D#:   I   V   I   V

Example 2. Debussy: *Nuages.*

This provides one clear instance in which the understanding of metric context influences harmonic interpretation.

Reference

Bregman, Albert. **Auditory Scene Analysis**. Cambridge: M.I.T. Press, 1990.

Ira Braus is in the Department of Music, Bates College, Lewiston, ME 04240; tel. (207) 786-6135.

Stephen Wu:

Automatic Arrangement of Popular Song Melodies

The project on automatic arrangement of popular song melodies (*CM91*, p. 116) is still under way. Local music arrangers were asked to suggest sets of heuristics for finding rhythmic patterns to accompany given popular song melodies. However, the responses did not prove to be especially useful, because in most cases they applied only to a few specific songs and did not apply generally to the repertory. Some respondents suggested that the pop music melodies should be divided into different classes (such as pentatonic, etc.) and that different sets of heuristics should be identified for each class. A method for classifying pop music melodies remains to be devised. Comments, ideas, and suggestions from overseas are now invited. Suggestions on heuristics for chord assignment to pop melodies are invited as well.

As a sideline of the project, "factors" of a pop song are now also being identified so that programs can be written to analyze a melody to see if there is any correlation between the factors and the melody's popularity.

The pseudocode and results of the rhythm-finding algorithm can be found in the paper "An Efficient Algorithm for Rhythm Finding," mentioned in *CM91*. It is scheduled to appear in the Summer 1992 issue of the *Computer Music Journal*.

Stephen Wu *invites comments and suggestions, which may be sent to him at the Department of Computer Science, University of Hong Kong, Pokfulam, Hong Kong; tel. +852 5/715 7466; e-mail: swu@csd.hku.hk.*

Eva Ferková:
Computer Analysis of Classic Harmonic Structures

Some algorithmic elements of a comprehensive system for automatic harmonic analysis of compositions in the classical style pose the need to articulate processes and concepts that are not well defined in most music theory treatises. A system under development at the Slovak Academy of Sciences is based largely on vocabulary and concepts prevalent in recent Central and Eastern European music theory. The algorithms of the analysis have been developed by musicologist Eva Ferková. The author of the programs, written in *Turbo Pascal* for MS DOS computers, is Marian Dudek. A commercial version of the program called *CACH* is available for PC compatibles [see *CM 1991*, p. 80]; Version 3 supports notational input and graphic and sound output.

CACH produces three kinds of analytical results: chordal analysis, functional analysis, and tonal analysis. Each series of labels is shown on a separate line beneath the music [see illustration with commentary in *CM 1990*, p. 117]. In order to obtain the correct output from the algorithm in response to the given input, it was necessary to clarify and introduce a number of principles, notations, and details. These are summarized below.

Chordal Analysis

The chordal analysis routine is based on the well-known principle of triadic structure. The first step is the identification of thirds of either 3 or 4 semitones. The superposition of the thirds is built up; every inversion of the chord is converted to root position. Then a look-up table is consulted. Seven kinds of chords—four types of triads (major, minor, augmented, and diminished) and three types of seventh chords—are currently identifiable. The latter are these:

D7	(dominant seventh chord, structure 4-3-3 semitones)
Zm7	(diminished seventh chord, structure 3-3-3 semitones)
Zmm7	(half diminished seventh chord, structure 3-3-4 semitones)

It is necessary to take into account not only the sizes of constituent intervals but also constituent tone names, particularly in the case of the diminished seventh chord, since every inversion of this chord has the same semitone structure.

Another problem was to find chords which are built up in a horizontal line, as in arpeggiations and the *style brisé*. The algorithm deals with chords in which some defining tones may be absent. A method is still being sought for the task of differentiating between accompaniment tones and melodic tones in the same chord.

Tonal Analysis

The first problem in the tonal analysis routine is to determine whether the primary key is major or minor. We rely here not only on the key signature, but also on the calculation of a *chordal weight*. It is derived from the quantitative and qualitative evaluation of the two possible tonic triads.

Chordal weight, which is used only for tonic triads, is determined by a scoring system which assigns values based on duration (1 point for a quarter-note value, 2 points for a half-note value, etc.). One point is added for each incidence of a triad in the first beat of the measure. The value obtained by summing all the values then constitutes the chordal weight. To further confirm the accuracy of the choice of the two possible keys, we also look for the sharp at the seventh degree of a minor key; the most frequently used minor in classical music was the harmonic minor key.

The assignment of tonal function (tonic, dominant, etc.) operates both globally [throughout the piece] and locally [within a modulatory passage]. However, the determination of the precise location in which the tonal center starts to change has proved to be difficult to define algorithmically. It was decided that the tone or chord in which a new local accidental is introduced must be considered as the most important location of possible key change. From the moment we consider an accidental to indicate a modulation, this is added to the key signature, and we look for another local accidental until the key signature is completed.

The name of the tonal center is expressed in the output by an inflection name (*x* for sharp, *b* for flat) and a tonal center name (C, D, E, F, G, A, H; or alternatively in lower case letters for minor keys).

Functional Analysis

The functional determination of the chords is based on the position of the root of every chord and its relationship to the center. The most basic task was to find the root and assign its scale degree.

It was more problematical to determine unambiguously the tonal function of a given chord in the modulating range. We have adopted a rule according to which each tone in the modulating range is most likely related to the following chord, and consequently, each chord is functionally evaluated according to its relationship to the following one (as tonic). It has been demonstrated that such an evaluation is possible only when at least one leading tone exists between the two examined chords (*i.e.*, a semitone distance between some tones of these two chords).

The harmonic and tonal plan is described only with the basic structures (seven types of chords; see below), and basic harmonic functions are described only when it is possible to find the root and the tonal center of the chord. It is not yet possible to describe other more complicated harmonic structures; therefore it is the goal of work in progress. It is possible to change the signs and names of the chords, key centers, and functions in the program according to the user's requirements.

Dynamic Potential

To evaluate the dynamics of harmonic formations, in connection with the graphic representation of the results, on 3 levels—chordal, tonal, and functional—the new concept of "dynamic potential" has been proposed. Its use in the program depends on three factors: the chord structure, the presence or absence of leading tones in consecutive chords, and tonal stability, including measures of distances between successive tonal centers. The numerical values for *chordal dynamic potential* are:

> 0 = major or minor triad
> 1 = augmented triad
> 2 = diminished triad, *D7, Zm7, Zmm7*
> 3 = compound chord without tritone
> 4 = compound chord with tritone

The numerical values of *functional dynamic potential* are then:

> 0 between two chords without any leading tone
> 1 between chords with 1 leading tone
> 2 between chords with 1 leading tone, when 1 chord lies
>   outside the tonality
> 3 between chords with 2 leading tones
> 4 between chords with 2 leading tones, when 1 chord lies
>   outside the tonality
> 5 between other chords

The numerical values of *tonal dynamic potential* are:

> 0 for a tonally specified range
> 1 for modulation to a like-named key (*e.g.*, from A major to A minor)
> 2 for modulation to a key a fifth higher or lower
> 3 for modulation to a key a third higher or lower
> 4 for modulation to a key a second higher or lower
> 5 for modulation to the key of the tritone

It is also possible to show chordal, functional, and tonal dynamic potential using graphs.

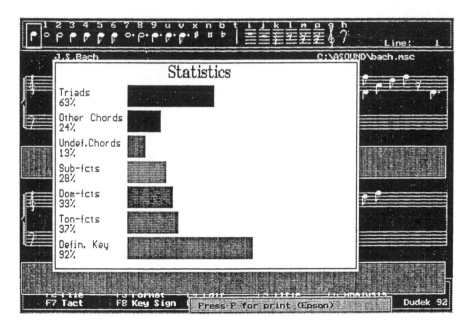

CACH: **frequencies of categorized harmonic events.**

Ways are presently being sought to expand the applicability of this approach to non-classical tonal music. Plans are also underway to develop a database of Slovak classical music which can be analyzed by the system.

The programs can be adapted to a broad range of applications, both analytical (*e.g.* in studies of stylistic characteristics) and educational. The concept of the automatic calculation of dynamic potential could provide a means by which to evaluate the harmonic pace of musical works.

References

Brusjanin, G.   "Osnovnoy ton slozhnykh akkordov" ["The Root of Compound Chords"] in *Problemy muzykal'noy nauki* [*Problems of Musicology*], 5 (Moscow, 1983).

Chalupková, V.   "Tonal Analysis of a Set of Songs and its Evaluation" [in Slovak] in *Musicologica Slovaca*, 6 (Bratislava, 1978).

Dudek, Marian.   "Interaktiny system na automatizovanu analyzu klasickej harmonie," ["An Interactive System for Automatic Analysis of Classical Harmony"]. Bratislava: MFF UK, 1990.

Ferková, Eva.   "Some Possibilities of Using the Computer in the Analysis of Melody and Harmony" [in Slovak]. Ph.D. thesis, Slovak Academy of Sciences, Bratislava, 1986.

Ferková, Eva.   "An Algorithm for Basic Harmonic Analysis of Tonal Classical Music" in abstracts of the conference *Computers in Music Research* (Queen's University, Belfast, 1991), pp. 66-68.

Filip, M.   *Laws of Development of Classical Harmony* [in Slovak].   Bratislava, 1965.

Janeček, K.   *Harmony through Analysis* [in Czech].   Prague, 1963.

Kresánek, J.   *Tonality* [in Slovak].   Bratislava, 1982.

Suchoň, E.   *Chords* [in Slovak].   Bratislava, 1979.

Zaripov, R. Kh.   *Kibernetika i muzyka* [*Cybernetics and Music*].   Moscow, 1971.

Eva Ferková is at the Ustav Hudobnej Vedy [Institute of Musicology] SAV, Fajnorovo Nabrezie 7, 81364 Bratislava, Czechoslovakia; tel. +42 7/720-003; e-mail: ferko@mff.uniba.cs.   She welcomes comments and queries and can provide a CACH demonstration diskette to prospective users.   Marian (Maros) Dudek is on the Faculty of Mathematics and Physics, Comenius University, 84215 Bratislava, Czechoslovakia.

Lelio Camilleri, Francesco Giomi, and Chiara Duranti:
Time Slices for Time-Span Reductions:
An AI Environment for the Analysis of Tonal Harmonic Structure

In a continuing series of experiments whose aim is to create an expert system for tonal harmonic analysis, the recent emphasis has been on integrating with other theoretical assertions the theoretical kernel used as the basis for the system. Based on the time-span reduction principles of Lerdahl and Jackendoff, this effort has come to address the analytical strategy and some weak points of this methodology.

Following from earlier work on computer algorithms to segment melodies (Camilleri *et al.*, 1990), we are now engaged in the testing of a harmonic lexicon parser and a rule system. First the system divides the piece into time slices, as in the underlying analytical methodology. The slices are catalogued according to their harmonic properties. At this stage the slices that are, in relation to a triadic chord, ambiguous or unconventional are given a probable interpretation and a label. Next the probable cadential points are determined. The software allows us to compare the skeleton of this probable "harmonic phrase structure" with some others internalized by the system. This part of the system is concerned with the representation of the structural properties of the "harmonic phrase."

After this surface analysis, the program then attempts to abstract the distinct hierarchical levels, moving to progressively more general levels of definition. The process is similar to the implementation of the segmentation rules which could influence more or less the generation of the hierarchical levels. For a precise model of selection processes, some analytical results can be influenced by several "certainty factors" by producing partially different paths and solutions. For example, when there is a rule conflict and the priority values of the conflicting rules are very similar, the system can perform two different analyses of the same piece, each producing a different degree of reliability.

The system is also designed to explain those lines of reasoning followed in making a decision. Sophisticated instruments (for example a "trace" with several levels of detail) are given to the user to solve this problem.

The implementation makes use of various rule-based techniques derived from the methods of artificial intelligence. The operational part of the program is written in *Pascal*; the facilities of the IBM ESE shell were particularly useful for speeding up the software development process. Forward and backward chaining as well as rule execution control statements were used.

References

Camilleri, Lelio, Francesco Carreras, and Chiara Duranti.   "An Expert System Prototype for the Analysis of Musical Grouping Structure," *Interface*, 19/2-3 (1990).

Lelio Camilleri, Francesco Carreras, and Francesco Giomi are in the Divisione Musicologica of CNUCE/C.N.R. and can be reached at the Conservatorio di Musica «L. Cherubini», Piazza delle Belle Arti, 2, 50122 Firenze, Italy; tel. +39 55-282105; fax. +39 55-2396785; e-mail: CONSERVA@IFIIDG.BITNET.

Stephen Malinowski:

Music Wheel

Music Wheel is a device for studying musical harmonies in real-time. The computer display consists of a circle which is divided into twelve "pie slices" corresponding to the twelve pitch classes, arranged in the order of the "circle-of-fifths." The display is controlled by a *MIDI* instrument, typically a keyboard. When notes are played, the corresponding slice of the circle is highlighted. This tool is useful for studying pitch sets, the nature of harmonic motion, etc.

As an enhancement, the circle is divided into three bands. The central band is highlighted whenever any note in a given pitch-class is sounding, giving the "now" state. The inner band gains intensity whenever a note in a specified pitch class is sounded, and decays slowly over time; this band shows which notes have been recently prevalent. The outer band is fully highlighted when a note in the corresponding pitch-class is sounded and decays quickly; this band, then, shows the most recently sounded notes, regardless of their prevalence.

*The **Music Wheel** has been developed for PC-compatibles by Stephen Malinowski, 1850 Arch St. #5, Berkeley, CA 94701; tel. (510) 548-9240; or c/o InnoSys, Inc., 2020 Challenger Drive, Ste. 101, Alameda, CA 94501; tel. (510) 769-7717; fax (510) 769-1953.*

David Evan Jones:

CPA: Counterpoint Assistant

Every pitch in rigorous common-practice counterpoint (a Bach fugue, for example) is subject to definable constraints in a matrix of (at least) two dimensions—the melodic and the harmonic. In a strict canon, for example, each pitch forms a part of a thematic pattern that recurs elsewhere in the texture, while that same pitch functions to further an independently varied series of harmonies. Twentieth-century composers such as Bela Bartók, Igor Stravinsky, and others have also constructed counterpoints according to their own rigorous melodic and harmonic constraints.

CPA [*Counterpoint Assistant*] is a composer's-assistant program for the Macintosh. It is written in *Allegro Common LISP*. It is designed to allow contemporary composers a maximum of control over a contrapuntal texture while assigning to the computer most of the calculation usually associated with rigorously controlled counterpoint.

The user specifies a harmonic template (a set of allowable chords in pitch-class notation) and a melodic template (a set of allowable lines of intervals [not interval classes]). The user then composes and enters a two-part counterpoint at the *MIDI* keyboard. In a strict canon, the allowable lines in the melodic template would be intervallically identical to or permutations of the original lines entered at the keyboard.

Lastly, the user specifies (1) the number of voices (up to 12) desired in the final texture, (2) whether the voices played at the keyboard are to be treated as inner voices or outer voices, and (3) the number of notes to be "offset" (*i.e.*, the number of pulses possible between the entrance of the first and last voices of the texture).

Incorporating the two voices played at the keyboard, *CPA* computes all of the possible realizations of a contrapuntal texture with the indicated number of voices where every note in the texture is both a constituent of one of the allowable melodic lines in the melodic template and also a member of one of the allowable chords in the harmonic template. Sometimes hundreds of realizations are possible; in other cases none are possible. The user may then play back the realizations, manipulate them in various ways, and select the ones to retain.

David Evan Jones *is in the Department of Music, University of California, Santa Cruz, CA 95064; tel. (408) 459-2951; fax (408) 459-3535; e-mail: dej@cats.ucsc.edu.*

Hermann Gottschewski:
Graphic Analysis of Recorded Interpretations

Since the Seventies the analysis of and theoretical discussion about recorded interpretation have grown to become a significant part of musicological research. As far as they include detailed analyses of sound recordings, most of these studies focus on (1) the relationship between interpretation and composition; (2) the relationship between several interpretations of the same composition; (3) delineation of interpretational schools and traditions; and (4) the grammar of interpretation, *e.g.* a rule-system for "musically" realizing a score. All these approaches deal with interpretation in relation to external factors such as notation, other interpretations, tradition, or theoretical constructs. While such research leads to interesting results, it does not deal with the crucial aesthetic problems of the impression of unity, of consistency, or of formal perfection in an interpretation. These qualities rely primarily on the inner relations of the interpretation itself rather than on relations to external conditions.

In order to provide an approximation to the understanding of formal perfection in interpretational art, one must consider the recorded interpretation as a structure in itself. This is not to ignore the structure of the composition, for structural relations within the composition appear as structural relations within the interpretation and can be recognized as such. If they do not, they have no relevance to the aesthetic quality of the interpretation. There is no better way to demonstrate the structural quality of an interpretation than to transform the relevant factors into a graph. Once the principles of transformation, (*e.g.* the selection of the features to be represented) and the design of the graph are chosen, the computer is a useful aid for measuring and editing the data and for printing the graph.

"Tempo structure" means the disposition of metrically hierarchical ordered time-points over a piece. The time-points are measured at the half-bar or quarter-bar level and are hierarchically grouped in units reflecting the musical structure. In most cases these are 1-, 2-, 4-, and 8-bar groups. Figures 1 and 2 [pp. 94, 95] represent two of four graphic types which can be constructed for analyzing tempo structures. Both illustrate the tempo motion, a characteristic which is strongly related to our musical experience, simultaneously at several levels. For example, it is possible to feel a steady pulse at a two-bar level, even if the one-bar and half-bar divisions are irregular and arbitrary. The program is written for MS-DOS compatible computers and a 24-dot printer with 1/180 inch resolution.

The first type of graphic representation is particularly appropriate to illustrate short-term tempo modifications. These are displayed so that a physically steady acceleration appears as a straight line. In Figure 1 the hierarchical phrase-structure of the Mozart exposition is reflected in Reinecke's interpretation in the hierarchical disposition of three kinds of "tempo bows": (1) accelerating, opening; (2) retarding, closing; and (3) symmetrical, perfect. These can be represented as follows:

The principle of data transformation is quite simple. Horizontally there is a real-time-axis with bar numbers for orientation. In Figure 1 the bar numbers are given according to the *Neue Mozart Ausgabe*. Carl Reinecke, in his recorded arrangement for piano solo (Welte-Mignon, 1905), changes the formal disposition of the exposition to be analogous to the reprise, while he leaves it unchanged in the printed edition of his arrangement.

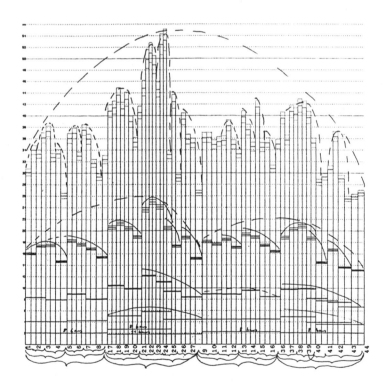

Figure 1. Carl Reinecke playing the exposition of the first movement of Mozart's piano concerto K. 537 in D Major (recorded for Welte-Mignon in 1905). Hierarchical phrase structure is shown by horizontal braces and "tempo bows" by dotted curves.

The vertical axis is a metronome scale in Figure [graph-type] 1 and a duration scale in Figure [graph-type] 2. Each relevant time interval in the tempo structure is displayed as a rectangle, standing on the real-time axis with the vertical sides at the beginning and the end of the time interval and with the height of its duration in the second case expressing the corresponding metronome value (*i.e.*, the reciprocal value of the duration in 1/minute) in the first case. All rectangles in the first graph have the same area, while all rectangles in the second graph have the same side ratio. If one would, in the second graph, choose the same scale for both axes, all rectangles would become quadratic.

Additionally in Figure 1 there are two auxiliary lines for the height of each rectangle. These mark an interval in which the true value most probably is located. This is because the data are measured from a Welte-Mignon piano-roll, where it is necessary to consider a certain inaccuracy of punching. This inaccuracy is only relevant for shorter intervals.

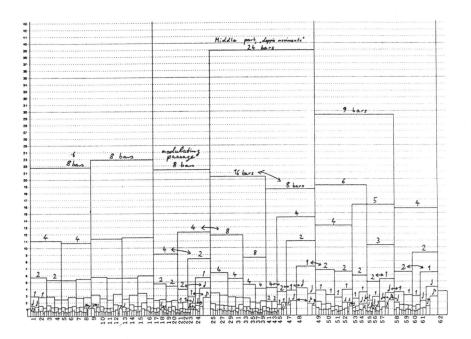

Figure 2. Saint-Saëns playing Chopin's Nocturne Op. 15, No. 2 in F# Major (recorded for Welte-Mignon in 1905).

The second type of graphic representation is useful to illustrate formal proportions and rhythmical phenomena. In Figure 2 one can see a real-time correspondence of parts with different quantities of bars at all levels: the 13-bar reprise has in real time the same length as the 16 opening bars; in the middle part the first 16 bars have nearly the same length as the following, strongly retarded 8 bars; within this ritardando, successively four bars, two bars, one bar, and a half bar have nearly the same length in real-time. Since such correspondences occur in almost all ritardando passages of this recording, it must be regarded as a structural device to give a ritardando phrase a convincing form.

....

Hermann Gottschewski is at the Musikwissenschaftliches Seminar der Albert-Ludwigs-Universität, Werthmannplatz, W-7800 Freiburg, Germany; tel. +49 761/203-2055; fax: +49 761/ 203-2056.

Emil H. Lubej:
A Portable Digital Acoustic Workstation in High Fidelity

Pursuit of the goal of developing portable equipment for ethnomusicological fieldwork has been enhanced by the advent of laptop computers. By connecting the laptop, if it has a suitable interface, with a digital recorder, one can store and analyze materials in the field and discuss preliminary results with the informants while still on location. This represents a significant advance over the former practice of doing the analysis at home long after the collection of data has been completed. A portable workstation combining a portable computer, printer, interface box, DAT recorder, casette recorder, and CD player was presented at the 31st World Conference of the International Council for Traditional Music, which was held in Hong Kong in 1991. A picture of the equipment is shown below. [Its modest size can be judged by comparison with the briefcase in the background.]

Photograph by Peter Cermak [used by permission]

In the workstation setup shown and described here, special software supports the analysis of pitch, timbre, tempo, etc. The equipment described below can also be used for text editing, database management, note processing, analysis of transcriptions (with *MAPPET* and *EMAP*), *MIDI*, and other tasks.

Various programs for ethnomusicological analysis of pitch, rhytm, timbre, and so forth, ranging from the simple graphical representation of the digital signal to a spectrogram with interactive measuring and selective auditory control, have been developed to run on this equipment. These programs form a second part of *EMAP* [*Ethnomusicological Software Package*].

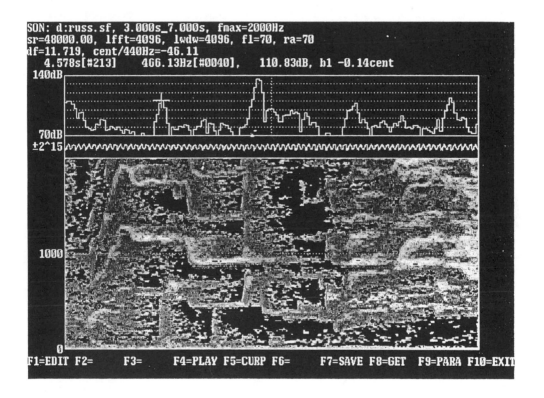

Screen running EMAP programs. At the top we see a spectrogram of a Russian song for female voices characterized by glissandi. The lower screen shows Fourier transforms on one section in florid polyphony. Transcription is facilitated by selective acoustic and numeric control.

The specifications are as follows:

1. Hardware

a. Computer: Toshiba T5200 (80386, 20MHz, 200Mb/15ms, Coprocessor, 8Mb RAM, 16bit full-length slot). For this application the hard disk must be large and fast enough because each second of a signal requires 196,000 bytes (48KHz * 16bit * 2 channels). There are only a few portable computers with this specification.

b. AD/DA-Converter: For the AD/DA conversion, the AIWA/HHB 1 PRO portable DAT recorder is used. It has a professional AES/EBU and a simple SPDIF digital I/O-interface with 32, 44.1, and 48Khz power supply, rechargeable [40-minute] battery or 10 alkaline batteries [good for three hours], which is very important for field research.

c. Interface: The *56K Digital Recording System* from Turtle Beach Systems is used as an interface. It consists of the 16-bit full-length 56K-PC Digital Signal Processor Card, which is based on the Motorola 56001 signal processor with 10.25 Mips/20MHz (now 33Mhz), and the *56K-D Digital Interface Box* with the I/O for the AES/EBU or SPDIF [image file] format, *MIDI*-In/Out [sound], and *SMPTE* [time stamping] for time codes.

2. Software: The 56K Digital Recording System includes the program *Sound Stage* to record, play, and edit signals in real time.

....

Emil H. Lubej *is at the Institut für Musikwissenschaft der Universität Wien, Universitätsstr. 7, A-1010 Wien, Austria; fax +43 1/402533; e-mail: A7321DAC@AWIUNI11.BITNET.*

Leigh Landy:
Categorization of Sound Transformations

In the first phase (1991) of a two-stage research project, sound transformations within electro-acoustic music have been treated primarily from a musicological point of view. An effort was made to describe what might be called the aesthetics (or dramaturgy) of

In the second phase (1992) a software environment for the creation of sound transformations is being prepared in conjunction with routines currently available through the Composers' Desktop Project based in York, England. The software is intended for use in composition and in the study of sound morphologies.

Leigh Landy is at the Institute for Musicology, University of Amsterdam, Spuistr. 134 Rm. 652, NL 1012 VB Amsterdam, The Netherlands; tel. +31 20/525-4446 (or -4443); fax +31 20/525-4429; e-mail: landy@alf.let.uva.nl.

Paul McGettrick:
Style and Variation in Irish Traditional Flute Playing

Stylistic variations of the performance of a traditional repertory provide the main focus of this study. Such features as rhythmic and melodic variation, ornamentation, and phrasing are primary concerns. The emphasis of the query is on the performing style rather than on the notated music.

To define variations between performances, fieldwork recordings are first entered into an IBM PC using the *SCORE* notation program. *SCORE*'s *PMX* command is used to create a separate parameter file for each tune file. This parameter file is an ASCII file in which every element of staff notation is numerically represented. A multi-purpose program written in *PCL* is then run. It first extracts from each parameter file only the numbers relevant to the analysis (*e.g.*, for pitch, duration, marks, etc.) and writes them to a new file. It then analyzes the new "filtered" files for various stylistic characteristics.

When complete, the program will guide new users through a variety of analysis options facilitating input of the name of a performer, tune, or musical feature and providing support for the inclusion of new parameter files in the database.

Paul McGettrick is completing a dissertation under the supervision of the Music Department, University College, Cork, Ireland; e-mail: ARAR6013@IRUCCVAX.UCC.IE. He is eager to hear from users working with the SCORE encoding system in an analytical framework.

Max V. Mathews:

The *Conductor* Program

The *Radio Baton*, a conducting apparatus, and the *Conductor* program which runs it are intended to facilitate more expressive performance with synthesizers and electronic instruments. Their further development is my main objective.

A prototype system using an embedded computer has been demonstrated in several places. The entire instrument including an embedded synthesizer will fit inside the square baton sensor box, which will itself fit on a small table or stand. The only required external equipment will be normal power amplifiers and loudspeakers.

The score that is conducted is provided by previously stored musical data. As this is fed to the instrument from a computer, the human conductor can control tempo, volume, timbre, and other parameters by moving the baton(s) in appropriate ways.

In the future, I believe that obtaining machine-readable scores for the Conductor Program will be the most important ongoing task. Data in three formats have now been successfully translated. These formats are *MIDI*, *SCORE*, and *MuseData* from the Center for Computer Assisted Research in the Humanities.

References

Mathews, Max V. "The Conductor Program and Mechanical Baton," *Current Directions in Computer Music Research*, ed. M. V. Mathews and John Pierce. Cambridge, MA: M.I.T. Press, 1989.

***Max V. Mathews** is at the Center for Computer Research in Music and Acoustics, Stanford University, Stanford, CA 94305; tel. (415) 723-5203; fax (415) 723-8468; e-mail: MVM@CCRMA. STANFORD.EDU. His and others' work on controllers was featured in Dan Phillips's article "The Control Freaks," Electronic Musician 8/6 (June 1992), 48ff.*

Stephen Malinowski:

Tapper

Tapper is an implementation of the conductor program described by Strangio (1977) and Mathews (1989). Previously stored *MIDI* data is released by real-time *MIDI* events generated by a keyboard. Each NOTE-ON MIDI performance event releases the next set of simultaneous NOTE-ON MIDI events (this could be either a single note or a chord). Each NOTE-OFF MIDI performance event releases the next set of NOTE-OFF MIDI events. Pedal (damper) MIDI performance events are passed through unchanged. Note velocity of performance events determines the velocity of the loudest playback event in the set; other events in the set are scaled to match the original data.

References

Strangio, C. E. "Computer-Aided Musical Apparatus and Method" (U.S. Patent 4,022,087, filed 1974, issued 1977).

Mathews, Max V. "The Conductor Program and Mechanical Baton," *Current Directions in Computer Music Research*, ed. M. V. Mathews and John Pierce. Cambridge, MA: M.I.T. Press, 1989.

Tapper has been developed by Stephen Malinowski, 1850 Arch St. #5, Berkeley, CA 94701; tel. (510) 548-9240; or c/o InnoSys, Inc., 2020 Challenger Drive, Ste. 101, Alameda, CA 94501; (510) 769-7717; fax (510) 769-1953.

Mary Simoni:

Temperament

Score files may be played in several different temperaments using the NeXT application called *Temperament*. This program may be used in conjunction with an archive containing information about the historical development of temperament on keyboard instruments. Pythagorean, Just, Mean Tone, Equal, Well, and Five & Seven [devised in 1987 by O. Jorgensen] are the tunings currently supported.

Mary Simoni *is in the Department of Music, University of Michigan, Ann Arbor, MI 48109; tel. (313) 764-1152; e-mail: mary_simoni@um.cc.umich.edu.*

Paolo Tortiglione:

FLUXUS

FLUXUS is a research project devoted to the development of a real-time musical workstation suited to applications in music analysis, synthesis, and performance. A multimedia interface will treat information presented as sound, images, text, and graphics. The research is based on a study of the nature of information and takes advantage of fundamental changes in hardware architecture facilitated by the development of the digital signal processing (DSP) chip 3210 [by AT&T]. It also takes into account the possibilities for desktop conferencing introduced by the development of an integrated digital service network (ISDN).

Paolo Tortiglione *can be reached at Viale Monte Penice, 10, I-20089 Rozzano (MI) Italy; tel. and modem: +39 2/8254066; e-mail: Paolo.Tortiglione@p9.f316.n331.z2.fidonet.org.*

Ulf Larnestam:

Simulation of Keyboard Sonata Movements
in the Style of Mozart

The aim of my present work is to make a generative study of sonata movements in the style of Wolfgang Amadeus Mozart and to examine the idea of mechanical composition, especially as described by Johann Georg Sulzer and Heinrich Christoph Koch. This work on musical simulation, which began six years ago, is focussed entirely on the first movement of eighteenth-century keyboard sonatas. Since it is known that Mozart was highly familiar with the music of Bach's youngest son, Johann Christian, some simulations of his music have also been attempted. The first movements that have been taken as models are those of Mozart's sonatas K. 284, 309, 311, 333, and 545 and of J. C. Bach's Op. 5, Nos. 2-4, which were arranged by Mozart in the concerto K. 107.

The dualistic view of musical creativity that prevailed in the eighteenth century distinguished between a mechanical side of composition, which did not demand "true musical insights," and an aesthetic side that did. The mechanical apparatus of composition was definitely seen to be of a lower order than the aesthetic. Sulzer goes so far as to call a composer lacking in artistic sensibilities a "note machine." This presumed mechanical level of composition makes the repertory of the period appear to be especially well suited to computer simulation.

Several programs are involved in my method of creating a simulation. The first program sets up instructions that determine the principal form, the texture types, and other fundamental information. The second automatically plans harmony and principal rhythms and suggests melodic contours. Through this stage no actual notes are generated; instead the program manipulates symbols (*e.g.*, for chords). A rule-oriented program then provides the actual notes, which must conform to standard compositional rules for dissonance treatment, avoidance of parallel fifths and octaves, and so forth. The output data is then converted to the format used by the notation program. The first four programs run on DOS machines. The programs have been developed from scratch using *PDC-Prolog* and its forerunner *Turbo Prolog* in conjunction with a music printing program, *Bella M*, developed in our department.

Some of the main variables in the program are the following:

> *form*: different kinds of periods and *Absätze* derived from Koch's theory of interpunctive form

phrase types: introductory, beginning, intermediary, modulatory, ending, cadential, closing, etc.

texture types: *e.g.*, melody in right hand with chords in left hand; more than 30 other types

harmonic types: specific plans and progressions described by harmonic function

accompaniment types: oscillating (including several "Alberti" types), figural, etc.

general melodic types: scale-based, figural (predominantly in sixteenth notes), etc.

A simulation of keyboard music by J. C. Bach: beginning of a first movement.

The process of composition is viewed as a concatenation of phrases. A phrase is defined to be a unit of either one or two bars of notated music. Each new phrase in its raw form is adjusted to suit the context that has unfolded in preceding phrases. In contrast to the *Würfelspiel* principle sometimes attributed to Mozart, in which phrase content is stored in a vocabulary, the phrase content is generated anew in this program. Some solutions are suggested by *Prolog* predicates, which involves randomization.

A simulation of keyboard music by W. A. Mozart: beginning of a first movement.

The question one hopes to answer concerns the degree to which "musical genius" that cannot be simulated by machine occurs in the natural repertory. This will be seen to be greater or lesser, depending on the competence of the algorithms used (Penrose, 1989).

References

Budday, Wolfgang. *Grundlagen musikalischer Formen der Wiener Klassik. An Hand der zeitgenössischen Theorie von Joseph Riepel und Heinrich Christoph Koch dargestellt an Menuetten und Sonatensätzen (1750-1790).* Kassel: Bärenreiter, 1983.

Cope, David. *Computers and Musical Style.* Madison, WI: A-R Editions, Inc., and Oxford: Oxford University Press, 1991.

Koch, Heinrich Christoph. *Versuch einer Anleitung zur Composition.* 3 vols. Rudolstadt (I) and Leipzig (II, III), 1782-93. Reprint: Hildesheim, 1969.

Penrose, Roger. *The Emperor's New Mind: Concerning Computers, Minds, and the Laws of Physics.* Oxford: Oxford University Press, 1989.

Ratner, Leonard. *"Ars combinatoria*: Chance and Choice in Eighteenth-Century Music" in *Studies in Eighteenth-Century Music: Festschrift for Karl Geiringer* (London: George Allen, 1970), 343-63.

Sulzer, Johann Georg. *Allgemeine Theorie der Schönen Künste in einzeln, nach alphabetischer Ordnung der Kunstwörter auf einander folgenen Artikeln abgehandelt,* 4th edn. Frankfurt and Leipzig, 1798. Reprint: Hildesheim, 1967.

....

*This research forms the subject of **Ulf Larnestam**'s doctoral dissertation in the Department of Musicology, University of Uppsala, Övre Slottsgatan 6, 753 10 Uppsala, Sweden; tel. +46 18/13-80-76; fax +46 18/12-09-54. His programs have been developed under the supervision of Prof. **Erik Kjellberg**.*

David Cope:

Pattern Matching as an Engine
for the Simulation of Musical Style

EMI (Experiments in Musical Intelligence) employs classical artificial intelligence (AI) pattern-matching techniques to emulate musical style. In *EMI*, pattern matching involves the setting of a variety of constraints limiting how accurately *EMI* allows one pattern to equal another; millions of combinatorial possibilities exist. Even small adjustments can be critical for style recognition to take place. Motives have a window component (tuning) which controls how many intervening notes occur before the motive counts. The ultimate list of motives becomes the "image" of the work (inclusive of vertical texture maps).

The tunings (of which "window" above serves as an example) include such parameters as:

> *threshold*: the number of increases before accepting the motive
> *allowance*: how much variation before a match can exist
> *length*: the number of pitches allowed in a motive
> *contour-levels*: determines the constraints on melodic shape
> *duration*: overall time length of a perceived motive

Other arguments which may or may not be needed to help refine signatures include *delete-window*, *order-shift*, *beat-relevance-to-match*, *dissonance-level-to-match*, *augmentation-variable*, *diminution-variable*, *parallel-key-shift*, and *inversion-recognition*, with each function intended to be made transparent by its name. Balancing the various tunings is an intuitive process utilizing musical experience and skills.

When a second work is analyzed and its subsequent image is overlaid on the first, those motives which significantly increase in number are considered the essence of the style of the composer and become signatures. Locations of each motive are noted for future composition. Those that increase somewhat but not substantially are considered to be *coercing agents*. The remaining material is determined as local to each work and is discarded.

A rules-base is adopted for structuring the voicing constraints (assumed to be tonal, if not otherwise specified); these are inherited by each object in the environment which governs all motion (with a signature override, if necessary). The rules-base includes

Music printed by *Professional Composer*.

***EMI*: A two–part invention in the style of J. S. Bach.**

doubling and succession rules (including those for chromaticism) found in property lists associated with the object vector names. An approximate texture-map formed during a sweep in the analysis imaging is then introduced into the object tree. While not conforming exactly to any single work by the composer under study, this map conforms to an average of input works. Signatures and biasing agents may override this mapping.

A new work is composed top-down, following a linguistic metaphor wherein the signatures are treated recursively as augmented transition networks, with a translation to MIDI (intervals to pitches) representing the final completion of the various programs. Parsed works vary due to the fact that at many given moments many possible correct answers exist. Hence new works in old forms may take the style of any composer given more than one work input, correct balancing of the tuning of the analysis, and foreknowledge of the requested form.

References

Prior to the publication of *Computers and Musical Style* (Madison, WI: A-R Editions, Inc., and Oxford: Oxford University Press, 1991), papers on *EMI* appeared in *IEEE Computer* (July 1991), *Interface* (1989), *AI Expert Magazine* (March 1988), and the *Computer Music Journal* (Winter 1987), as well as in the proceedings of the *First International Workshop on Artificial Intelligence and Music* (Bonn, September 1988), the *Sloan Conference on Computing and the Humanities* (Dartmouth College, 1988), the annual meeting of the *American Association of Artificial Intelligence* (St. Paul, August, 1988), the symposium *Charles Ives and the American Music Tradition up to the Present*, and the *International Computer Music Conference* (1987).

David Cope *can be reached at Porter College, #88, University of California, Santa Cruz, CA 95062; tel. (408) 459-3417; e-mail: howell@cats.ucsc.edu.*

Ioannis Zannos:

The *Momus* Music Generation System

A music generation system combining algorithmic and cognitive approaches is now being developed. The purpose of this research is to provide composition tools which are understandable in perceptual and cognitive terms, rather than simply in abstract algorithmic ones.

The basic constituents of the systems are a "minimal musical language" and a "pitch-time net." The first is a kind of musical assembler with a very simple instruction set. Its basic data item is a single bit, and the instructions handle data registers, a stack for nested execution of loop statements and go-tos, memory, and I/O [input/output] ports.

Several "minimal processors" together are needed to define the movement of a single musical "voice," or just part of a voice, in the pitch-time net. The pitch-time net is a net whose points represent numbers of fixed relationships in each dimension. Distance in the net is proportional to a measure of complexity of rational numbers, as proposed by Euler and modified by Vogel (1984). This in turn expresses the perceptual relationships or distance of tones and of durations. It is thus possible to define the consonance of intervals and of chords, as well as the "distance" between chords and tonal regions (following algorithms developed by Vogel and Draaf [1984, 1988]). As a principle for music generation, the idea of balance in the movement and in the shapes corresponding to the notes of a piece in the pitch-time net is examined. Thus the system can be metaphorically likened to an "animat" or small robot, moving in the space, with the purpose of restoring or maintaining balance in the shapes it is creating by its movement.

The output of the minimal processors is like nerve signals to individual muscles. The processors must be coordinated to give the desired movement, a problem receiving much attention in robotics.

The system is programmed in the object-oriented graphic programming environment *MAX* (created at IRCAM for the Macintosh and now distributed by Opcode Systems) and extended by user-defined objects written in *THINK C.* Several virtual processors can run at the same time.

The output of the algorithmic part is fed into the connectionist part. This processes the temporal structures of its input by means of a number of subsystems which evaluate the cognitive properties of rhythmic, harmonic, and melodic structures. The subsystems are modeled on current research work on music cognition and music analysis by Martin Vogel (evaluation of the consonance of chords), Lerdahl and Jackendoff (grouping and hierarchical structure of music), Povel and Essens (perception of temporal patterns), and others. The musical examples used to develop the model are from Western tonal music and also from Near-Eastern modal music. A sample piece is shown below.

HÜZZAM BESTE

Momus: One example (of the *beste* genre of Turkish vocal music) used to develop a model of Near-Eastern composition. This piece is in the *Hüzzam* mode and was written in the nineteenth century by the composer Bekir Agha.

References

Draff, M. "Eine neue Fassung der Klangschrittformel" in *Colloquium Festschrift Martin Vogel* (Bad Homet, 1988), 51-60.

Lerdahl, Fred, and Ray Jackendoff. *A Generative Theory of Tonal Music*. Cambridge: MIT Press, 1983.

Maes, Pattie (ed.). *Designing Autonomous Agents: Theory and Practice from Biology to Engineering and Back*. Amsterdam: Elsevier Science Publishers (North Holland), 1990.

Povel, Dirk-Jan, and Peter Essens. "Perception of Temporal Patterns." *Music Perception* 2(1985)/4, 411-440.

Vogel, Martin. *Anleitung zur harmonischen Analyse und zu seiner Intonation (Orpheus: Schriftenreihe zu Grundfragen der Musik*, 34). Bonn—Bad Godesberg: Verlag für Systematische Musikwissenschaft, 1984.

Ioannis Zannos is conducting this research as part of a dissertation thesis in Information Engineering at RCAST, Ohsuga-Hori Laboratory, University of Tokyo, 4-6-1 Komaba, Meguro-ku, Tokyo 153, Japan; e-mail: iani@ohsuga.rcast.u-tokyo.ac.jp.

Christine Roueche:

Hypermedia, Advanced Database Systems, and Cognition: The Development of a Multi-faceted Aid to Musicological Research

Because documents relevant to musicological research are both dispersed and heterogeneous, two problems are commonly encountered in their study. First, it is difficult to access different types of information, and, second, sources of information are qualitatively different. These sources may comprise (1) texts, for example biographies of authors, circumstances of creation, comparison between sources, or criticisms of the period studied; (2) images, such as incipits or scores; and (3) sounds, including specific interpretations of a musical work. Our objective is to devise an electronic environment that will take all these factors into account and provide combined access to these diverse kinds of information.

In our system, we intend to take into consideration works of musicians of the seventeenth and eighteenth centuries. Our project is related to the work of the Centre de Musique Baroque de Versailles as described in *Computing in Musicology 1991* (p. 33).

Modern documentary techniques rely on diverse kinds of musical thinking, which we hope to explore and accommodate. Cognitive categories might take into account the nature of the relevant dimensions by which a musical work is structured, perceived, and analyzed. While pitch and rhythm are significant for traditional means of analysis of Western music, a cognitive approach may help to clarify notions such as timbre and style. Our belief is that any system conceived for research purposes should allow the user to deal with specific knowledge as it is related to these categories. We intend to take into account the way users usually search for information and resolve problems. In sum, our system aims at helping musicologists undertake their search as naturally as possible.

Consequently, our knowledge base has to be highly interactive and has to handle not only static but also some dynamic phenomena. For example, users could ideally change plans or objectives in the process of searching without giving up the main plan or goal, or they could set up requests combining their own choice of parameters. The system should, for instance, enable the user to ask for simple or polymodal documents, such as a score and the critiques related to it, to do some type of analysis on the score, such as searching for the repetition of a motive while taking into account adequate variations, and more generally to formulate either simple or structured requests.

In order to achieve our objectives, we decided to study the association of object-oriented and deductive databases, hypermedia systems, and a knowledge representation language. The first allows us to deal with large amounts of multimedia documents and to manage the different kinds of requests needed, the second one offers the possibility of a more natural way of retrieving information (the user can navigate throughout the base), and the last one provides efficient means of structuring the knowledge base.

Christine Roueche *can be contacted at the Laboratory of Artificial Intelligence and Cognitive Sciences, École Nationale Superieure des Telecommunications de Bretagne, BP 832, 29285 Brest Cedex, France; tel. +33 98/00 14 28; fax: +33 98/00 12 82; e-mail: roueche@enstb. enst-bretagne.fr.*

Bernard Bel, Jim Kippen:
Identifying Improvisation Schemata with QAVAID

QAVAID, the Urdu word for grammar, is an acronym meaning *Question-Answer Validated Analytical Inference Device*. It is the name that has been given to a machine-learning software product designed by Bernard Bel (*Centre National de la Recherche Scientifique*, Marseille) in collaboration with ethnomusicologist Jim Kippen (University of Toronto), with support from the International Society for Traditional Arts Research (ISTAR). The prototype runs under *Prolog II*, an extension of the Prolog language developed by *Groupe Intelligence Artificielle* (Marseille II University). A compiled version is under development.

Given a set of (positive) instances of some unknown language L, *QAVAID* is able (1) to build a grammar/automaton recognizing exactly the sample set, (2) to infer a proper segmentation of sentences, and (3) to propose generalization rules by which the grammar is able to recognize and/or produce a language containing the given examples and new sentences belonging to L. This process is incremental, meaning that a hypothetical grammar and segmentation are upgraded each time a new example is supplied. This inductive inference technique is meant to overcome the shortcomings of knowledge acquisition in rule-based systems such as the *Bol Processor* (see *CM 1991*, pp. 78f).

QAVAID assumes that the sample set is error-free and that language L is finite (although its alphabet is not necessarily predefined). Sentences in a finite language are concatenations of a small number of "words", *i.e.* a vocabulary that may be used for segmenting sentences. Since several equivalent context-free grammars may rely on different vocabularies, the problem (in the absence of semantic information) is to find one that yields a relevant segmentation. Additional knowledge is therefore necessary. In the domain of percussion "languages," expert musicians seem to be able to make reliable decisions regarding segmentation when prompted to compare solutions (consistent with the information they previously supplied). An important methodological point is that this dialogue with the machine makes explicit the minimum amount of background knowledge needed for inferring a proper grammar and segmentation from a given sample set (Kippen and Bel 1989).

Generalizing a grammar requires strategic knowledge such that "evident" generalizations are envisaged first. Partial ordering of generalizations in *QAVAID* is based on our experience with grammars representing improvisations on a compositional type called *qa`ida* in North Indian *tabla* drumming.

ISTAR France and the Faculty of Music at Toronto University are setting up a project on improvisation in contemporary drum music. *QAVAIDs* will also be used by anthropologist David Turner of the University of Toronto in his fieldwork on Australian Aboriginal songstreams.

An Example of the Learning Process

Sentences below are onomatopoeic transliterations of the first lines of ten variations of a *qa`ida* using alphabet {dha, tr, kt, ge, ti, dhee, na -}. Symbol "-" is a silence, and "tr" and "kt" are pronounced "tira" and "kita" respectively.

dha tr kt dha	tr kt dha ge	dha ti dha ge	dhee na ge na
dha tr kt dha	tr kt dha dha	dha ti dha ge	dhee na ge na
dha ti dha tr	tr dha tr kt	dha ti dha ge	dhee na ge na
dha tr kt dha	ti - dha ti	dha ti dha ge	dhee na ge na
dha tr kt dha	ti dha tr kt	dha ti dha ge	dhee na ge na
ti - dha ti	dha dha tr kt	dha ti dha ge	dhee na ge na
ti dha tr kt	dha dha tr kt	dha ti dha ge	dhee na ge na
tr kt dha ti	dha dha tr kt	dha ti dha ge	dhee na ge na
tr kt tr kt	dha dha tr kt	dha ti dha ge	dhee na ge na
tr kt dha tr	kt dha ge na	dha ti dha ge	dhee na ge na

This set can be produced/recognized by the finite-state automaton

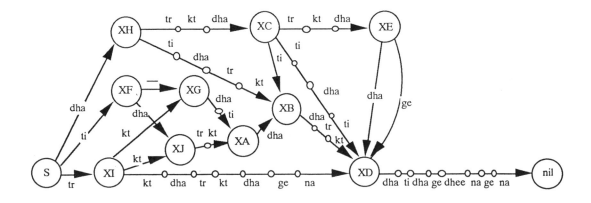

which is equivalent to the context-free grammar:

S	—>	TE1 XI
XI	—>	TA7 XD
XD	—>	TA8
XI	—>	TF1 XJ
XJ	—>	TC2 XA
XA	—>	TA1 XB
XB	—>	TB3 XD
XI	—>	TF1 XG
XG	—>	TB2 XA
S	—>	TA1 XH
XH	—>	TF4 XB
XH	—>	TA3 XC
XC	—>	TE4 XD
XC	—>	TA3 XE
XE	—>	TA1 XD
XE	—>	TC1 XD
XC	—>	TB1 XB
S	—>	TB1 XF
XF	—>	TA1 XJ
XF	—>	TD1 XG

TA7	—>	kt dha tr kt dha ge na
TC2	—>	tr kt
TE1	—>	tr
TF1	—>	kt
TF4	—>	ti dha tr kt
TD1	—>	-
TB2	—>	dha ti
TE4	—>	ti - dha ti
TC1	—>	ge
TB3	—>	dha tr kt
TA8	—>	dha ti dha ge dhee na ge na
TA3	—>	tr kt dha
TB1	—>	ti
TA1	—>	dha

Rules in the right column highlight expressions that have been repeated several times in the sample set, presumably "words" of the language. In fact, this vocabulary and the derived segmentation are not acceptable. A proper inference requires the supervision of an informant answering questions about segmentation. The detailed dialogue for this sample set may be found in Kippen and Bel (1989). The grammar obtained in this way is:

S	—>	TA3 SA13
SA13	—>	TA3 SA10
SA10	—>	TC2 SA8
SA8	—>	TD2 SA6
SA6	—>	TA6
SA10	—>	TA2 SA8
SA13	—>	TC5 SA8
SA13	—>	TD2 SB11
SB11	—>	TA3 SA8
S	—>	TB2 SA14
SA14	—>	TD2 SA12
SA12	—>	TA2 SB10
SB10	—>	TB2 SA8
S	—>	TE2 SA14
S	—>	TF2 SB14
SB14	—>	TB2 SA12
S	—>	TB2 SB14

S	—>	TB2 SC14
SC14	—>	TA3 SA11
SA11	—>	TB3 SA8
S	—>	TD2 SD14
SD14	—>	TA3 SB11
TB3	—>	dhagena
TF2	—>	tidha
TE2	—>	ti-
TC5	—>	dhati-dhati
TA6	—>	dhagedheenagena
TD2	—>	dhati
TC2	—>	dhage
TA3	—>	dhatrkt
TB2	—>	trkt
TA2	—>	dhadha

To generalize this grammar, *QAVAID* will enlist states of the equivalent automaton that may be merged or connected with new paths. Domain-dependent knowledge limits the number of states to be considered: since all sentences must have identical lengths, two states are eligible only if they denote suffix sequences of equal lengths. In the grammar above, the state mergings to be considered are: SA11 = SB11, SD14 = SA14, SD14 = SB14, SD14 = SC14, SB10 = SA10, and SA14 = SB14 = SC14. In *QAVAID*'s strategy the last merging will be envisaged first because of the three production rules

S ——> TB2 SA14   S ——> TB2 SB14   S ——> TB2 SC14

that make it reasonable to suppose that suffix sequences derived from SA14, SB14 and SC14 are similar since they share TB2 as a prefix. *QAVAID* also determines pairs of states that may be connected via new paths using the known vocabulary. This amounts to substitution of permuting words of equal lengths such as: *trkt / dhati / ti- / tidha / dhage / dhadha* and *dhatrkt / dhagena*. Thus, using background knowledge, the search space for possible generalizations is considerably reduced: only eight out of 132 pairs of states will be examined, among which three are considered more significant.

References

Bel, Bernard. "Inférence de langages réguliers," Proc. *Journées Françaises de l'Apprentissage (JFA 90)*, (Lannion, 1990), 5-27.

Bel, Bernard. "Acquisition et représentation de connaissances en musique." Ph.D. dissertation, Université Marseille III (1990).

Bel, Bernard. "Modelling Improvisatory and Compositional Processes," *Languages of Design— Formalisms for Work, Image, and Sound,* 1. Amsterdam: Elsevier, 1992.

Kippen, Jim. "Where does the End Begin? Problems in Musico-cognitive Modelling," *Minds and Machines*, 1 (1992).

Kippen, Jim, and Bernard Bel. "The Identification and Modelling of a Percussion 'Language' and the Emergence of Musical Concepts in a Machine-learning Experimental Set-up," *Computers and the Humanities*, 23/3 (1989), 199-214.

Kippen, Jim, and Bernard Bel. "A Pragmatic Application for Computers in Experimental Ethnomusicology" in *Research in Humanities Computing 1: Papers from the 1989 ACH-ALLC Conference,* ed. Susan Hockey and Nancy Ide, guest ed. Ian Lancashire (Oxford: Oxford University Press, forthcoming).

Bernard Bel *can be contacted at GRTC, CNRS, 31 ch. J. Aiguier, F-13402 Marseille Cedex 09, France; fax: +33 91/71 08 08; e-mail: bel@grtc.cnrs-mrs.fr;* **Jim Kippen** *can be reached at the Faculty of Music, Edward Johnson Building, University of Toronto, Canada M5S 1A1; fax: (416) 97 5771; e-mail: kippenj@epas.utoronto.ca.*

Francesco Giomi, Marco Ligabue:

A Cognitive Approach to the Analysis of Electro-acoustic Music

To address the problem of the individuation and definition of sound objects in electro-acoustic music for the purposes of analysis we have been exploring the use of an aesthetic-cognitive approach to the description of such objects. The process begins with the definition of a phonematic paradigm and continues with the individuation of analytical-computational strategies. The proposed methodology starts from the theoretical assumption that the sound object is a moneme, *i.e.*, a primary unit of articulation. This unit is constituted by phonemes (secondary articulation units) capable of functioning as distinctive features. On balance this is a predominantly aesthetic approach. In our case, all the traits were considered distinctive, because each one can create, from a perceptive point of view, a specific differentiation among distinct sound objects.

Most of the categories we employ are Schaefferian ones, even though we carried out some selections and integrations. We eliminated the redundant or less functional categories from the analytical-descriptive point of view, adding some others we considered useful to accomplish the task. These included duration, relative dynamic level, co-textual weight, spatial position, and so forth. After formalizing the paradigm of distinctive features, we made a series of computational tables based on the phonological method "present feature/absent feature (+, -)" which facilitates description and comparison.

We used two types of automatic table comparisons. The first type describes single sound objects: this comparison is diachronic. The second type brings together homogeneous elements from the typological or morphological point of view: this comparison is synchronic. The successive comparison of the tables makes possible the analytical process. It allows us to verify the direct or transverse composer's strategies during the organization of sound events. Thus it is possible to produce results that are interesting from the structural point of view as well.

We hope to extend this research to include sound-events recognition and comparison by means of neural networks.

References

Chion, Michel. *Guide des objets sonores*. Paris: INA-GRM/Buchet-Chastel, 1983.

Giomi, Francesco, and Marco Ligabue. "Analisi assistita al calcolatore della musica contemporanea." Rapporto Interno C92-01. Pisa: CNUCE/C.N.R., 1992.

Giomi, Francesco, and Marco Ligabue. "An Aesthetic-cognitive Approach to the Description of the Sound Object. From the Definition of a Phonematic Paradigm to the Individuation of Analytical-computational Strategies." *Semiotica* [forthcoming].

Schaeffer, Pierre. *Traité des objets musicaux*. Paris: Editions du Seuil, 1966.

Francesco Giomi and *Marco Ligabue* are in the Divisione Musicologica CNUCE/C.N.R. and may be reached at the Conservatorio di Musica «L. Cherubini», Piazza Belle Arti, 2, 50122 Firenze, Italy; tel. +39 55-282105; fax. +39 55-2396785; e-mail: CONSERVA@IFIIDG.BITNET.

Catherine Stevens:

A Temporal Back-Propagation Neural Network
for the Study of Music Recognition by Human Listeners

A recently completed series of experiments using musically trained and untrained subjects provides evidence for feature extraction and feature weighting processes in the recognition of short tonal and atonal compositions (Stevens, 1992). The experiments were cast within a pattern-recognition framework and used discrimination and classification tasks wherein such melodic and temporal features as interval magnitude, melodic contour, rhythm, tempo, transposition, closure, and modality were manipulated and investigated. Both kinds of subjects were able to perform the discrimination and classification tasks, although in general musically trained subjects performed significantly better than untrained subjects in terms of recognition speed and accuracy.

Connectionist or artificial neural network models (*e.g.*, by Rumelhart and McClelland, 1986; Jordan, 1986; Kohonen, 1988; and Lang, Waibel, and Hinton, 1990) are presently being developed to further explore feature extraction and weighting processes in music recognition (Bharucha and Todd, 1989; Gjerdingen, 1990; and Leman, 1990). The facilitatory effect of musical training has been conceptualized in our connectionist models as the efficient assignment of weight to features of musical compositions.

Musically trained subjects, as a result of their experience with musical stimuli, possess efficient strategies in the extraction and differential assignment of weight to features. Untrained subjects, on the other hand, are not so efficient in weight assignment and therefore respond slowly and less accurately than trained subjects. Connectionist models can be exposed to a musical environment and trained to an optimal level of performance to simulate "expert" or trained subjects, whereas models which are given less training or exposure to a musical environment can be used to simulate "novice" or untrained subjects. In this way, direct comparison can be made between the recognition performance and feature extraction and weighting processes in connectionist models and those of human subjects who have been set the same tasks.

Connectionist models which simulate music discrimination and classification tasks have been developed on Macintosh SE and IIci computers using the neural network simulation package *MacBrain 3.0.* Most recently, a two-layer back-propagation network which permits sequential input of melodic information has been designed. The input units of the network were divided into time slices corresponding to the number of tones in the composition and, during training, scaled frequencies activated each time slice in sequence. A network consisting of 21 input units and a single output unit has been trained to discriminate between atonal sequences on the basis of interval magnitude and rhythm, and a network comprising 71 input units and two output units has been successfully trained to classify tonal melodies according to melodic contour.

These connectionist models are now being used to generate further hypotheses about music recognition processes. For example, activation values of output units over time, and the connection strengths or weights on input and output units can be directly compared with the recognition times recorded by human subjects. Preliminary analyses reveal similarities between the activation values and weighting patterns in the connectionist models and the recognition times obtained from musically trained subjects. Hypotheses generated from the connectionist models about music recognition processes now await further experimental investigation and validation using musically trained and untrained listeners.

References

Bharucha, Jamshed J., and Peter Todd. "Modeling the Perception of Tonal Structure with Neural Nets," *Computer Music Journal*, 13 (1989), 44-53.

Gjerdingen, R.O. "Categorization of Musical Patterns by Self-organizing Neuronlike Networks, *Music Perception*, 7 (1990), 339-370.

Jordan, Michael I. "Serial Order: A Parallel Distributed Processing Approach." Technical Report No. 8604. University of California at San Diego, Institute for Cognitive Studies, 1986.

Kohonen, Teuvo. "An Introduction to Neural Computing," *Neural Networks*, I (1988), 3-16.

Lang, Kevin J., Alex H. Waibel, and Geoffrey E. Hinton. "A Time-Delay Neural Network Architecture for Isolated Word Recognition," *Neural Networks*, 3 (1990), 23-43.

Leman, Marc. "Emergent Properties of Tonality Functions by Self-Organization," *Interface*, 19 (1990), 85-106.

Rumelhart, David E., and James L. McClelland. *Parallel Distributed Processing: Explorations in the Microstructure of Cognition.* Vols. I and II. Cambridge, MA: MIT Press, 1986.

Stevens, Catherine. "Connectionist Models of Musical Pattern Recognition" in the *Proceedings of the Third Australian Conference on Neural Networks* (Department of Electrical Engineering, Australian National University, Canberra, February 1992), pp. 17-20.

....

Catherine Stevens is in the Department of Psychology at the University of Sydney, Sydney, New South Wales 2006, Australia; tel. +61 2-692-3227; fax 2-692-2603; e-mail: kates@psychvax. psych.su.oz. She can provide additional details on experimental design and connectionist modelling aspects of this project. See also the report in **CM 1991**, pp. 89-91.

Stephen Malinowski:

Music Animation Machine

The *Music Animation Machine* is a software program which creates a scrolling, bar-graph score from *MIDI* performance data. In essence it produces a score for viewers. Note timing is represented by horizontal position, at display resolution. Pitch is shown discretely by vertical position, with twelve note positions per octave. The scrolling of the score is synchronized with a *MIDI*-generated performance, such that the center point of the display corresponds to the "now" time. To further aid the viewer in correlating the image with the sound, the bar of color representing a given note brightens when the note is sounding.

Because this notation is completely graphical and non-symbolic, and because it is presented simultaneously with the music it represents, it is very easy to follow. Non-musicians and young children have little difficulty following the score, anticipating sounds which are about to be heard, etc. In addition, *MAM* provides a vehicle for explaining scoring, texture, velocity, and arguably tonality to those who do not read conventional notation. It is thus of potential value in the teaching of music appreciation as well as for rehearsal, visual analysis, and experimentation. Some viewers find its effect pleasantly hypnotic.

Color can be used to indicate pitch-class, using a circle-of-fifths coloring; this reveals harmonic structure, dissonance, and modulation. A horizontal compression feature causes frequently occurring pitches to be especially conspicuous. Conversely, the pitches of atonal music tend to appear evenly dispersed on the screen, with no apparent clustering. The performance editor requires an IBM PC-compatible computer, a Roland MPU-401 *MIDI* interface, a US video-recordable VGA graphics board, a trackball, a *MIDI* keyboard, and *MIDI* sound-production modules. The *MIDI* keyboard is used for input, which may be of voices played one at a time or by all parts simultaneously.

A number of editing functions are supported. Among these, the ratio of horizontal distance to time can be adjusted to any value, display colors can be changed on a note-by-note basis, and tempo and dynamics can be adjusted.

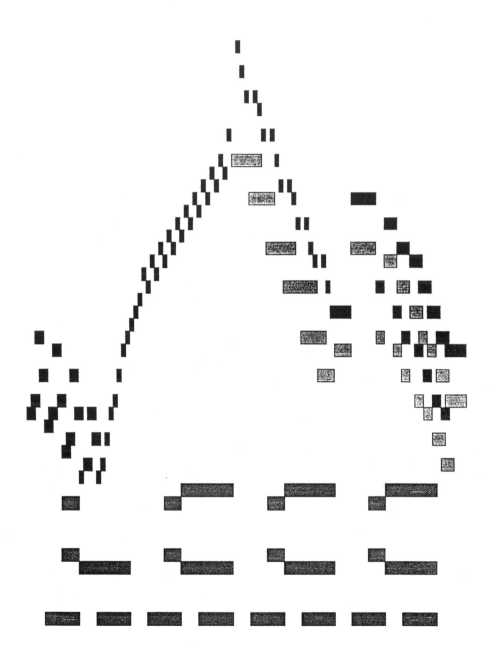

Music Animation Machine: an excerpt from Chopin's *Berceuse (1845).*   The horizontal bars at the bottom represent a left-hand ostinato, while the right-hand part, shown above, captures one of a series of elaborate variations (Bars 20-23).

A sample video tape of works created with *MAM* includes pieces, principally for keyboard, by Domenico Scarlatti, William Byrd, J. S. Bach, Beethoven, Chopin, and Webern.

The **Music Animation Machine** *has been developed by Stephen Malinowski, 1850 Arch St. #5, Berkeley, CA 94701; tel. (510) 548-9240; or c/o InnoSys, Inc., 2020 Challenger Drive, Ste. 101, Alameda, CA 94501; tel. (510) 769-7717; fax: (510) 769-1953.*

Chris Sansom, Laurence Glazier:
Fractal Music

Fractal Music is a software package for the Atari ST series of computers, written by Chris Sansom with advice and assistance from Laurence Glazier. The creation of this program began purely as a personal project. Sansom, a composer interested in mathematics and computing, was introduced to fractals by Glazier, a mathematician and computer programmer interested in music. Sansom conceived the idea of generating music from a fractal algorithm but rejected the "escape time" type of algorithm (as used, for instance, to generate the Mandelbrot set) in favor of one that would generate music in "real time" and in three dimensions (time, pitch, loudness); complex numbers are inherently two-dimensional.

The algorithm found to be most suitable employs trigonometrical functions to produce a new note/rest on every iteration, with each of the three new values (time, pitch, loudness) depending on all three values from the preceding iteration.

A compromise is involved where time is concerned: although pitch and loudness values may increase or decrease relative to their predecessors, this is not true of time. Therefore a positive x movement is taken to produce a note and a negative a rest, in which case the other two values produced on this iteration are ignored. The user can set a parameter which reverses this process (*i.e.*, negative → note, positive → rest). These two "versions" of the music may then be combined to form a continuous stream. A user in Australia, Robert Martin, suggested assigning the two versions to different voices, tuned a quarter-tone apart, thus making a valid use of a 24-note scale.

The music is realized by means of *MIDI*, which understands only integers. Further calculations must therefore be made on the results of the basic algorithm in order to produce meaningful music. What has been referred to here as "loudness" is generated as *MIDI* key-velocity. This is generally programmed to produce variations in loudness, but may, in some voice patches, change other parameters, such as brightness or vibrato.

The music which results shares many of the characteristics of what is generally recognized to be music: (1) coherence of rhythm and phrase and (2) near (but never exact) repetitions of melodic shapes. This last is also a central characteristic of visual fractals, usually referred to as "self-similarity."

After producing these results, Sansom felt the need to manipulate the music further. The program therefore includes some processing functions. Most of these are relatively commonplace (quantization, augmentation/diminution, inversion, retrograde), but Sansom also took the opportunity to extend his idea of rotating music through (or reflecting it in) any angle.

The program was entirely rewritten using *HiSoft Basic*, a sophisticated compiled BASIC for the Atari ST, and making full use of the *GEM* environment. The program is also compatible with the Standard MIDI File format, so that music from other programs can be manipulated in *Fractal Music*. The program's own output can be exported to a sequencer.

Chris Sansom *and* **Laurence Glazier** *can be contacted at Datamusic, 57 Cricketfield Road, London E5 8NR, England; tel.* +44 81/985 5268; *fax* +44 81/985 5268. *The program* **Fractal Music** *is available by mail order and fax from the above address.*

Further information about fractal relationships in music and other contributions on this subject are found in **CM 1991**, *pp. 92-101.*

Donald Sloan:

HyTime/Standard Music Description Language and Computer-Aided Music Research

The American National Standards Institute (ANSI) committee X3V1.8M has been working on two concurrent and related projects: the *Standard Music Description Language* (*SMDL*), which has been described in this directory in previous years, and the *Hypermedia/Time-based Document Structuring Language* (*HyTime*). These two projects have been given project numbers by the International Standards Organization (ISO). *SMDL* (ISO/IEC DIS 10743) contains most of what was previously described as *SMDL*, namely that which is specific to the music world.

HyTime (ISO/IEC 10744: 1992) contains the time model that originated in *SMDL*, as well as extensive facilities for integrating multimedia (including music), and linking objects for hypertext, hypermedia, and other purposes. HyTime has been approved as an international standard; the work on *SMDL* is still continuing. The division of *SMDL* and *HyTime* was necessitated by the potential for non-musical uses of time-based multimedia and hypermedia; in effect, *SMDL* uses everything in *HyTime*, then adds a number of facilities exclusive to music applications. That way, those who did not use music could adopt *HyTime* without the additional trouble of conforming to music functions that they would not use.

As might be expected with a project as complex as this, there have been a number of questions that the music community has asked and continues to ask. This article aims to address some of these questions, in order to give the music community a better idea of what *HyTime/SMDL* is and what benefits will come from its adoption.

In the 1990 issue of *Computing in Musicology* (pp. 53-56), Neill Kipp and Steven Newcomb provided a short excerpt written in *SMDL*, so that readers could get an impression of what a such a representation might entail. It would be misleading, however, to compare a few lines of code such as this:

```
<ces pitchgam = pitchgam 0>
<ce --( Ma- )-->
<musicdur> <vtu> 1 2 </vtu> </musicdur>
<note> <nompitch> <gampitch> <octave>2</octave>
    <pitchnam>e</pitchnm> </gampitch> </nompitch> </note>
</ce>
```

with other representations such as *DARMS*, *SCORE*, the CCARH *MuseData* format, or any other data content notation that can render this in a form that is more parsimonious and easier for musicians to read directly. The reason why such a comparison is irrelevant is because the *SMDL* code will likely never be seen by a musician who is encoding music in *SMDL*. It is expected that there will be software tools developed to create an attractive interface, so that the musician may input in a manner that he or she finds comfortable, without ever having to see something like the code listed above. The only persons who would need to deal with this code would be software developers making such tools. Furthermore, the example above need not take up as many bytes as it appears; there would be a large amount of markup minimization, a way of giving shorthand notation to reduce the bulk.

Even so, is there any particular reason why *SMDL* needs to be more verbose than other systems? The answer is complicated and lies in its relationship with an existing ISO standard, *SGML* [*Standard Generalized Markup Language*; ISO 8879], a widely used standard in the industrial and government publishing industries. In return for the extra complexity, one gets great flexibility in what *SMDL* may represent. It has mechanisms for containing other types of notations, for example. It would be possible within a single *SMDL* document to contain both *DARMS* and *SCORE* encodings of the same piece, with appropriate links to map information from one to another, insofar as is possible. For those cases in which another representation scheme contains information that is unintelligible to *SMDL*, there is a way of tagging the data as being part of that particular data content notation; this can potentially be resolved at a later time by a mechanism which can understand such notation.

There is great potential for efficient and thorough data searches with *HyTime/SMDL*. Consider one instance of a pitch or motive search. Below we see the representation of a pitch for a single note in *SMDL*:

```
< note > < nompitch > < gampitch > < octave >  2  < /octave > < pitchnm >  e
< /pitchnm > < /gampitch > < /nompitch > < /note >
```

This pitch representation is taken from the example above. For this example, the pitch depends on a resource called a pitch gamut, which is like a table listing the different notes of a scale. There is, by the way, a mechanism for chromatic alterations of scale degrees. As with other representations, the pitch name or register can be queried directly, as it is contained in the description above.

In addition, because of the structure of the gamut, one can write a query that also accesses the scale degree easily. In fact, one can perform transpositions simply by changing the pitch gamut, with the other relationships left intact. Since *SMDL* is based on the existing *SGML* standard, many mechanisms for data searching already exist and can be adapted for use with *SMDL*.

Since many of the existing representations can do much of what is described above, why is another representation necessary? While some music representations (*e.g.* *DARMS*, *SCORE*, CCARH *MuseData* format, etc.) capture the various aspects of a musical score and other representations (*e.g. MIDI*) focus primarily on capturing certain performance information, none of the systems predating *HyTime/SMDL* can combine both the score and potential performances in a coordinated manner, while making it clear which set of information is part of the core of abstract information and which is particular to each edition of a score or individual performance. This is an important feature of *HyTime/SMDL*, as the domain of core material (called the RcantusS in *SMDL*) exists separately from any visual or aural domain.

As an example of the usefulness of this feature, imagine a CD-ROM which contains a score to a Beethoven piano sonata, as well as three different performances. The program may coordinate the score with each performance, even though the timing of each may be completely different. In fact, there may even be an interactive feature to allow the user to add rubato to Serkin or to speed up Gould, since the user can refer to moments in the score; these would be linked to actual digital samples of each performance. Why use one format for the score (*e.g.*, *SCORE*), another for the performance (*e.g. MIDI*), and yet another for their interaction (CD-I)?

Aside from the actual features of *HyTime/SMDL*, it is important at this time to have a standard among the different music representations. With the proliferation of many different music representations, there has recently arisen a need to have translators between these various notations. With only a few notations, this is not a great problem. For example, if there were three representations, there would be a need for six translators to and from each pair. With ten representations, however, the number of translators required grows to ninety! The existence of a standard such as *HyTime/SMDL* would require only 20 translators in the latter case; one each to and from *SMDL*.

References

Newcomb, Steven R., Neill A. Kipp, and Victoria T. Newcomb. "The 'HyTime' Hypermedia/ Time-based Document Structuring Language," *Communications of the Association for Computing Machinery*, 34/11 (Nov. 1991), 67-83.

Donald Sloan is in the Department of Music, Ashland University, Ashland, OH 44805; tel. (419) 289-5113.

Stephen Travis Pope:

MODE and *SMOKE*

MODE [*Musical Object Development System*], a software system, and *SMOKE* [*Smallmusic Object Kernel*], a companion representation system, are oriented toward composition, performance, and analysis. Both are available free via anonymous file transfer [see below].

MODE 1.1, a re-implementation of the *HyperScore ToolKit*, is a collection of software class libraries for building musical applications. It is meant to be used with *Objectworks/Smalltalk 4.1* (by ParcPlace Systems, Inc.). The default release will run on a Sun SPARCstation and supports *MIDI* and high-quality stereo audio input and output. Versions of the *MIDI* and sound interfaces for Macintosh computers are expected soon. *MODE* includes such programming facilities as a music representation language, schedulers and drivers, user interface components, and built-in applications for editing and browsing. It also contains end-user applications for digital signal processing.

SMOKE's emphasis is on musical objects; it grows out of a *Smalltalk-80* environment and is best suited to implementation in *Smalltalk*, *LISP*, or *C++*. *SMOKE* has evolved from discussions principally involving researchers at Stanford (CCRMA) and Berkeley (CNMAT) and those participating via electronic mail with the alias *smallmusic@xcf. Berkeley.edu*.

SMOKE aims to provide a description language that supports abstractions and generalizations that form the foundations of music theory and composition. Among the features it would like to accommodate are abstractions of quantity (pitch, duration, dynamic level), events, textures, event-tree structures for description of parallel and sequential phenomena (parts, tracks, threads), and converters between data formats.

```
"Terse MusicMagnitude Creation using post-ops"
    440 Hz                           250 msec
    1/4 beat                         'c#3 pitch'
```

```
"Terse Events using concat. of music mags"
    440 Hz, 1/4 beat, -12 dB, (#voice --> #flute).
    38 key, 280 ticks, 56 vel.
    (#c4 pitch, 0.21 sec, 0.37 ampl).
```

```
"Terse EventLists using concat. of events or (duration --> event) associations"
    (440 Hz. (1/1 beat), 44.7 dB), "comma"
    (1 -> ((1.396 sec, 0.714 ampl) word: #xu))
```

```
"Bach Example—First measure of Fugue 2 from WTL (ignoring the initial rest)."
```

```
(((0 beat) -> (1/16 beat, 'c3' pitch)),
 ((1/16 beat) -> ('b2' pitch)),
 ((1/8 beat)  -> (1/8 beat, 'c3' pitch))),
((1/4 beat) -> ('g2' pitch)),
((3/8 beat) -> ('a-flat2' pitch)),
((1/2 beat) -> ((1/16 beat, 'c3' pitch)),
 ((1/16 beat) -> ('b2' pitch)),
 ((1/8 beat)  -> (1/8 beat, 'c3' pitch))),
((3/4 beat) -> ('d3' pitch)),
((7/8 beat) -> ('g2' pitch))
```

```
[Can be abbreviated further....]
```

[N. B. Parentheses in SmallTalk do not conform
to the practice of other computer languages.]

SMOKE: **A terse representation of Bar 1 of the C-Minor Fugue from J. S.
Bach's** *Well-Tempered Clavier*, **Book I.**

A musical surface can be represented as a series of events, each of which can have named properties of arbitrary value. These properties can be music-specific objects. Events can be grouped into lists; event lists can be nested into tree structures. [Screen displays of *MODE* event-list and tree-structure editors are shown on p. 132.] Events can belong to more than one list.

The amount of detail captured in these representations can vary. In amplification of the *terse* representation of the opening phrase of the Bach fugue shown above, a *verbose* representation might include information about dynamics, accent, *MIDI* equivalents, and so forth. A score in *SMOKE* consists of one or more parallel or sequential streams of event lists whose events may have interesting properties and links.

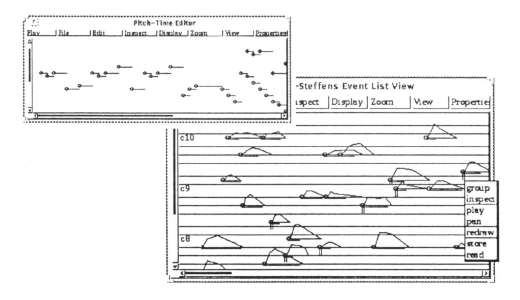

MODE: event-list editors.

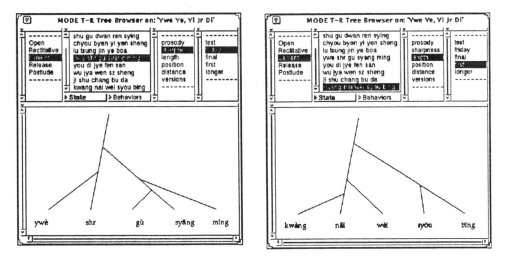

MODE: structure editors.

Stephen Travis Pope *edits the* **Computer Music Journal.** *He can be reached at PO Box 60632, Palo Alto, CA 94306; e-mail: stp@ccrma.stanford.edu.* **MODE 1.1** *is available via the Internet from the directory pub/st80 on the server ccrma-ftp.stanford.edu. Extensive documentation on* **SMOKE** *is available from the file reading.smalltalk.t in the same directory [anonymous @ccrma.Stanford.edu:/pub/st80].*

Bruce McLean:

An Editing System for Analysis of Musical Scores

An interactive system to assist analysis of tonal and serial scores is currently under development. The primary musicological objective is to map developmental process in scores by means of markers and textual annotations that may be attached to a score representation and also correlated among themselves. None of the analysis is accomplished computationally. The first set of test scores for the annotation system prototype consists of Beethoven's sonatas Op. 10, Nos. 5, 6, and 7. In support of the annotation component there is a limited query capability. It can display a designated location in a score; the location may be identified by a marker name, a time index value, or a simple musical notation pattern. This work is being carried out on a Macintosh IIci. Software is being developed with a *C* compiler (Symantec). Score data is encoded and entered in *DARMS* code.

Associated tasks include the encoding of scores and computer-unassisted analyses as well as the creation of (1) an internal representation, (2) data structures to support search operations, (3) retrieval language for location lookup, (4) an editing language for annotation entry, and (5) interfaces for display of musical notation and generation of audio realization of the score. Both output types will be available as either an unannotated score or musical excerpts associated with markers and annotations.

The feasibility of interfaces to facilitate other applications and remote access is also under examination. Among these possibilities are (1) a possible interface to *Finale* or other commercial application to provide *PostScript* files for printing, and *MIDI* files for audio output; (2) network conferencing protocols by which two or more geographically separated analysts could collaborate on an analysis with reference to the same displayable annotated score data, and (3) relative advantages of various temporally-augmented relational object-oriented, or custom database frameworks for storage, access, query, editing, and presentation in computational musicology.

It is anticipated that *DARMS* data or binary score structures will be available by modem beginning in October 1992, that a software-prototype system without score display or sound generation will be available in mid-1993, and that analytic results will be available by mid-1994. All dates are provisional and subject to change.

....

Bruce McLean *can be reached at Cantus Computing, Inc., 9975 Connell Road, San Diego, California 92131; tel. (619) 271-7150; fax (619) 271-0380; e-mail: bruce@cantus.com.*

Su-Yuen Ling:

Annotating Machine-Readable Scores

A method for annotating machine-readable music for later retrieval from a database is currently under development at Carnegie Mellon University. In the context of indexing tree-structured data in databases, each piece of music, whether a score or performance, will be represented by a tree in the system to be implemented. In the preliminary design, nodes in a tree denote sections, phrases, or notes. The user writes down relationships between nodes in order to specify the desired tree and thus retrieve the music that it represents.

Su-Yuen Ling *may be reached at the School of Computer Science, Carnegie Mellon University, Pittsburgh, PA 15213; tel. (412) 268-3828; e-mail: lingsy@cs.cmu.edu [Internet] or lingsy%cs.cmu.edu@carnegie [Bitnet] or ...!seismo!cs.cmu.edu!lingsy [UUCP].*

Jonathan Berger:

The *Intelligent Music Stand*

A project to create *The Intelligent Music Stand*, a network of computer terminals that can provide graphic display of musical materials in a stored database, is under development at the Center for Studies in Music Technology at Yale University. A "conductor" master stand will generate parts for individual performers. The project is based on the NeXT environment.

Jonathan Berger *may be reached the Center for Studies in Music Technology, School of Music, Yale University, New Haven, CT 06520; tel. 203/432-4264; e-mail: jberger@alice.music.yale.edu.*

Musical Notation Software

Edmund Correia, Jr.:

Annual Survey

Each spring CCARH sends out to approximately 75 developers of musical notation software a packet of musical examples containing passages which are problematic from a typographical point of view while being essential from a musicological perspective. The developers have a window of two to three months in which to respond with their own settings of the selected examples. The solicitation is accompanied by a form requesting specific information about the hardware and software environment in which the program is run. This information is used in compiling the short descriptions that appear at the end of this section.

The biggest change that we have noticed in the contributions of the past two years is related to the emergence of a class of expert users of particular programs who provide value-added service to those who would rather not go to the trouble of learning all the in's and out's of a notation program. This year, for example, Jeffrey Dean shows off his extensions to *Finale* for mensural notation, Don Giller extracts proportional notation using *Music Engraver* with *Adobe Illustrator*, and John Gibson produces a Schenkerian analysis using *Nightingale* and *Illustrator*.

A new approach in this year's contributions is taken by Bill Schottstaedt, who makes his *PostScript*-compatible program for notation available by FTP [for an explanation of FTP, see the article "Using Networks"]. As a non-commercial program, it provides no fancy manuals or telephone support, but in being available free of cost, it may have some appeal to the recession-weary. The programs originate on a NeXT workstation. Preliminary elements of another notation program, *MUZIKA*, are available from an FTP site in Israel.

A firm called Kallisti Music Press informs us in an advertising mailer that the "economic advantages of desktop publishing enables us...to offer [parts] for sale at prices below the rental rates of other publishers." The press, located at 810 S. St. Bernard St., Philadelphia, PA 19143, publishes works from the American repertory of the nineteenth and twentieth centuries. They call attention to a fundamental shift underway in the entire process of music publishing.

* * *

Over the eight years in which we have made this solicitation, the quality and availability of programs to print music have been enormously increased, but some of the issues in which users take the most interest remain incompletely addressed. Readers of

CM are therefore encouraged to consult earlier volumes to get a more complete picture of these issues.

Developers often report in detail on those aspects of their products that are especially competitive. Heavily advertised products that are listed but not shown here are missing because no contribution has been made. We also include mention of products that we learned of too late to include in our solicitation, especially if we believe they may be of value in the setting of difficult repertories. Some printing capabilities built into broad-spectrum *MIDI* programs are not oriented toward the needs of classical music. In consequence, these programs are represented only if such a capability is demonstrated. Much of the software for printing classical music comes from small firms with few employees. Inconveniently timed illnesses, manpower shortages, equipment failures, or relocations may prevent them from responding punctually.

Since no information is provided here on the human interface of each program represented, the difficulty of duplicating the illustrations is a separate matter from assessing the quality of the output. Readers are urged to test programs personally before buying them. All developers are virtuosos at operating their own programs!

Comments on the Illustrations

Rather than continue the trend toward greater and greater complexity in selecting the musical examples to be set for this year's issue, we thought a return to simpler musical times might be appreciated by our contributors. Accordingly, only two excerpts were chosen: a brief segment from the first movement of Beethoven's *"Archduke" Trio*, and a stretch of operatic recitative from Handel's *Ottone*, where the entrance of a character marks the beginning of a new scene. For variety, free choices were strongly encouraged, particularly of pre-1600 or post-1900 repertory.

In chamber works including piano, the pianist's part is generally printed on a standard-size grand staff, with all other parts shown on reduced staves. To exactly reproduce our Beethoven example, four different note sizes—two each for principal notes and grace notes—are required. Three sizes of clef signs are also needed. While most will probably agree that these distinctions give the best appearance, about half of the settings contributed let fewer suffice.

At first glance, the recitative excerpt may seem wide open and uncomplicated, but because of widely varying syllabic lengths, the rhythmic sense can easily be distorted if note placement is allowed to be determined solely by the text. The typesetter can help the singer achieve rhythmic accuracy here by adjusting the notes with respect to the text so that the distances between them more closely reflect their time values. A couple of our contributors particularly excelled in this regard, producing readily "singable" results. The use of various font sizes can also aid in clarifying the different levels of information: text, character names, stage directions, scene breaks, etc.

We remind our readers that the contributors are not required to duplicate the exact layout of our examples. They are free to choose the number of measures per system and the spacing of staves and systems, and even to shorten the excerpts somewhat in order to meet our space restrictions. Further reduction is often necessary on our part to allow for margins and headers.

List of Illustrations

The numbered illustrations are arranged (1) chronologically by composer and (2) alphabetically by the surname of the contributor. Illustrations are unretouched. Printer designations identify the specific configuration used to produce the example. Most programs can interface with several printers and some run on multiple platforms, but the results are not necessarily uniform. The originating hardware is indicated in this listing.

Handel: *Ottone* (1723), Act I, Scene 9.

1.	Excerpt distributed	
2.	Macintosh	*Nightingale*
3.	Macintosh	*Finale*
4.	IBM PC-AT	*COMUS music printing software*
5.	IBM PC	*The Note Processor*
6.	Macintosh II	*Music Engraver/Illustrator*
7.	Acorn Archimedes (PC)	*Philip's Music Scribe*
8.	Erato workstation	*Erato Music Manuscriptor*
9.	IBM PC	*The Copyist*
10.	IBM PC	*SCORE*
11.	UNIX workstation (Sun SPARC)	*MusE*

Beethoven: *"Archduke" Trio,* Op. 97 (1811): Allegro moderato.

12. Excerpt distributed
13. Macintosh   *Finale*
14. IBM PC-AT   *COMUS music printing software*
15. IBM PC   *The Note Processor*
16. Macintosh II   *Music Engraver/Illustrator*
17. Acorn Archimedes (PC)   *Philip's Music Scribe*
18. Erato workstation   *Erato Music Manuscriptor*
19. UNIX workstation (NeXT)   *CMN (Common Music Notation)*
20. IBM PC   *The Copyist*
21. IBM PC   *SCORE*
22. UNIX workstation (Sun SPARC)   *MusE*

Free choices—Macintosh:

23. Chopin Etude--a Schenkerian analysis   *Nightingale*
24. Mensural notation   Extensions to *Finale*
25. Proportional notation   *Music Engraver/Illustrator*
26. Mozart: Trio in F   *Lime*

Free choices—IBM PC compatibles:

27. Beethoven: Quartet in C# Minor   *Personal Composer*

Free choices—NeXT:

28. Mahler: Symphony No. 3   *CMN*

The listing of *Current and Recent Contributors* begins on p. 169.

Gallery of Examples

Illustration 1

Handel: *Ottone*, Act I, Scene 9

SCENE 9   Gismonda and the aforesaid

#23 Recitativo: Indietro, indietro!

The last system may be omitted if necessary.

Excerpt sent to software developers.

Illustration 2

Contributor: Donald Byrd   **Output from:** Linotronic L-300
Product: *Nightingale*   **Size as shown:** 95% of original
Running on: Apple Macintosh   **Engraver:** John Gibson

SCENE 9   Gismonda and the aforesaid

#23 Recitativo: Indietro, indietro!

Illustration 3

Contributor: Jeffrey Dean

Product: *Finale*

Running on: Apple Macintosh

Output from: Linotronic (2400 dpi)

Size as shown: 100% of original

Illustration 4

Contributor: John Dunn

Product: *COMUS* music printing software

Running on: IBM PC-AT

Output from: HP LaserJet+

Size as shown: 100% of original

SCENE 9   Gismonda and the aforesaid

#23 Recitativo: Indietro, indietro!

Illustration 5

Contributor: Stephen Dydo
Product: *The Note Processor*
Running on: IBM PC compatibles

Output from: Linotronics
Size as shown: 90% of original
Engraver: Susan Altabet

Illustration 6

Contributor: Don Giller
Product: *Music Engraver/Illustrator*
Running on: Apple Macintosh II

Output from: Linotronic 300
Size as shown: 100% of original

per- te   io pri-ma a- scen-do,   e di tua de-stra i - vi il bel do-no at- ten-do. Sten-di la bian-ca

SCENE 9   Gismonda and the aforesaid

#23 Recitativo: Indietro, indietro!

GISMONDA   ADELBERTO   GISMONDA

ma - no.   In - die-tro,   in - die-tro! Co - me! tu vie-ti o ma-dre... Ah!   que-sta,

[gli prende
la spada]   ADELBERTO GISMONDA

que-sta strin-ger tu dei. La spa-da? Non è tem- po di noz- ze, o mol-le a - man- te, ben tel pre-

TEOFANE ADELBERTO   GISMONDA

dis- si: Ot- to- ne è in Ro-ma! Ot- to- ne? Il   po- po- lo...   In-co - stan-te già il tuo ne-mi-co ac-

Illustration 7

Contributor: Philip Hazel   **Output from:** Apple Laserwriter
Product: *Philip's Music Scribe*   **Size as shown:** 100% of original
Running on: Acorn Archimedes (PC)

SCENE 9   Gismonda and the aforesaid

#23 Recitativo: Indietro, indietro!

Illustration 8

Contributor: Jeffrey L. Price
Product: *Erato Music Manuscriptor*
Running on: Erato workstation

Output from: HP LaserJet II
Size as shown: 95% of original

Illustration 9

Contributor: Crispin Sion
Product: *The Copyist*
Running on: IBM PC compatibles

Output from: QMS PS 800+
Size as shown: 70% of original

parte   io pri-ma_a - scen - do   e di tua de- stra i-vi_il bel do- no_at- ten do. Sten- di la bian-ca

6

SCENE 9   Gismonda and the aforesaid

#23 Recitativo: Indietro, indietro!

GISMONDA   ADALBERTO   GISMONDA

ma- no.   In - die - tro, in - die - tro! Co- me!   tu vie- ti_o ma- dre...   Ah!   que - sta,

4
2   6

[gli prende   ADALBERTO   GISMONDA
la spada]

que- sta strin- ger tu dei.   La spa- da?   Non e tem- po di noz- ze,   O mol- le_a man- te,   ben tel pre-

Illustration 10

Contributor: Leland Smith
Product: *SCORE*
Running on: IBM PC compatibles

Output from: NeXT laserprinter (400 dpi)
Size as shown: 50% of original

SCENE 9   Gismonda and the aforesaid

#23 Recitativo: Indietro, indietro!

Illustration 11

Contributor: Rolf Wulfsberg

Product: *MusE*

Running on: UNIX workstation (Sun SPARC)

Output from: Linotype L-300 (1270 dpi)

Size as shown: 100% of original

SCENE 9 Gismonda and the aforesaid

23. Recitativo: Indietro, indietro!

Illustration 12
Beethoven: *"Archduke" Trio*, Op. 97

Excerpt sent to software developers.

Illustration 13

Contributor: Jeffrey Dean
Product: *Finale*
Running on: Apple Macintosh

Output from: Linotronic (2400 dpi)
Size as shown: 100% of original

Illustration 14

Contributor: John Dunn

Output from: HP LaserJet+

Product: *COMUS* music printing software

Size as shown: 100% of original

Running on: IBM PC-AT

Illustration 15

Contributor: Stephen Dydo
Product: *The Note Processor*
Running on: IBM PC compatibles

Output from: Linotronics
Size as shown: 95% of original
Engraver: Susan Altabet

Illustration 16

Contributor: Don Giller

Product: *Music Engraver/Illustrator*

Running on: Apple Macintosh II

Output from: Linotronic 300

Size as shown: 100% of original

Illustration 17

Contributor: Philip Hazel   **Output from:** Apple Laserwriter
Product: *Philip's Music Scribe*   **Size as shown:** 100% of original
Running on: Acorn Archimedes (PC)

Illustration 18

Contributor: Jeffrey L. Price
Product: *Erato Music Manuscriptor*
Running on: Erato workstation

Output from: HP LaserJet II
Size as shown: 70% of original

Illustration 19

Contributor: Bill Schottstaedt
Product: *CMN (Common Music Notation)*
Running on: UNIX workstation (NeXT)

Output from: NeXT laserprinter (400 dpi)
Size as shown: 90% of original

Illustration 20

Contributor: Crispin Sion
Product: *The Copyist*
Running on: IBM PC compatibles

Output from: QMS PS 800+
Size as shown: 70% of original

Illustration 21

Contributor: Leland Smith

Product: *SCORE*

Running on: IBM PC compatibles

Output from: NeXT laserprinter (400 dpi)

Size as shown: 50% of original

Illustration 22

Contributor: Rolf Wulfsberg   **Output from:** Linotype L-300 (1270 dpi)
Product: *MusE*   **Size as shown:** 100% of original
Running on: UNIX workstation (Sun SPARC)

Illustration 23

Contributor: Donald Byrd
Product: *Nightingale*
Running on: Apple Macintosh

Output from: Linotronic L-300
Size as shown: 90% of original
Engraver: John Gibson

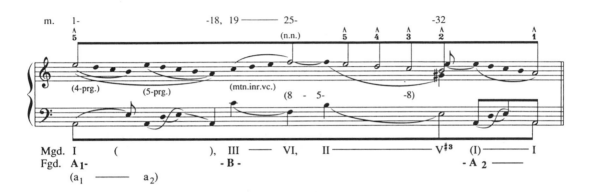

Schenkerian analysis of Chopin: *Étude*, Op. 10, No. 2.

Illustration 24

Contributor: Jeffrey Dean
Product: Extensions to *Finale*
Running on: Apple Macintosh

Output from: Linotronic (2400 dpi)
Size as shown: 100% of original

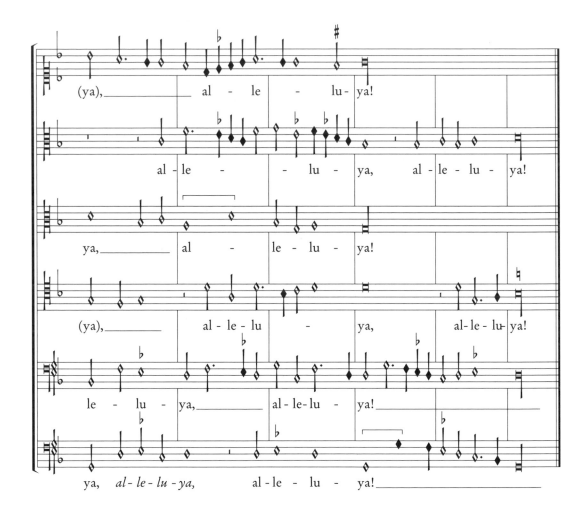

Mensural notation in Jo. Brunet: *Victimae paschali laudes*, bars 187-92.

Illustration 25

Contributor: Don Giller
Product: *Music Engraver/Illustrator*
Running on: Apple Macintosh II

Output from: Linotronic 300
Size as shown: 110% of original

Ban

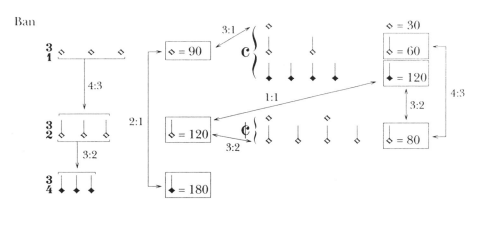

Mersenne

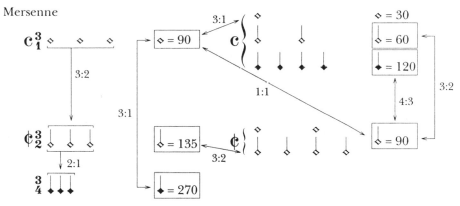

This example is reproduced from Paul Brainard, "Proportional Notation in the Music of Schütz and His Contemporaries," *Current Musicology*, 50 (1992).

Illustration 26

Contributor: Lippold Haken
Product: *Lime*
Running on: Apple Macintosh

Output from: Laserprinter
Size as shown: 80% of original

Excerpt from Mozart: Trio for Violin and Piano in F Major, K. 57.

Illustration 27

Contributor: David Moore
Product: *Personal Composer*
Running on: IBM PC compatibles

Output from: Laserprinter (300 dpi)
Size as shown: 70% of original

Excerpt from Beethoven, String Quartet in C# Minor, Op. 131, first movement.

Illustration 28

Contributor: Bill Schottstaedt

Product: *CMN (Common Music Notation)*

Running on: UNIX workstation (NeXT)

Output from: NeXT laserprinter (400 dpi)

Size as shown: 90% of original

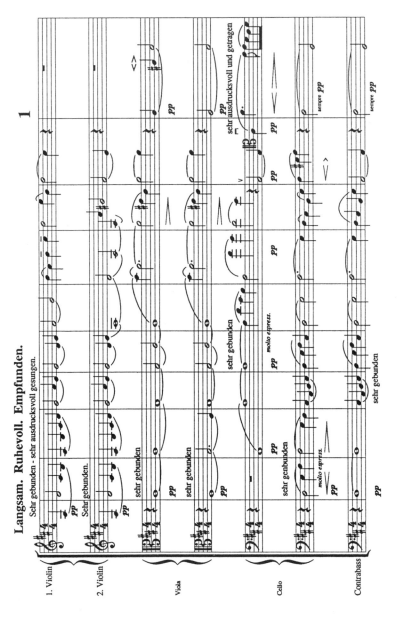

Beginning of final movement of Mahler: Symphony No. 3 in D Minor.

Current and Recent Contributors

This listing concentrates on systems that have been represented by illustrations over the past three years and incorporates definitions of terms needed to understand the accounts given. Additional systems that are now dormant were cited in earlier issues. Several developers (and their products) who have not contributed in recent years can be found in the 1990 volume of *CM*, pp. 62-73. Music printing programs advertised in popular music magazines are listed here if they have a demonstrated capability for handling classical music of moderate complexity.

A-R Music Engraver. See *MusE*.

Alpha/TIMES. Rehetobelstr. 89, CH-9016 St. Gallen, Switzerland; tel. +41 71-35-1402. An integrated input and analysis system by Christoph Schnell for the Apple Macintosh line. Illustrated in 1988 and previous years.

Amadeus. Amadeus Music Software GmbH, Rohrauerstr. 50, Postfach 710267, W-8000 München 71, Germany; tel. +49 89-7854750. This product, originally developed by Kurt Maas, is commercially available for the Atari Mega ST4 or TT. Both alphanumeric and *MIDI* input are supported, the latter facilitating acoustical playback. Most data are stored as ASCII files. Screen editing is provided. Output (for dot matrix and laser printers, plotters, and phototypesetters) is scalable to a resolution of 1000 dots per inch. Illustrated in 1991 and preceding years.

Berlioz. Logiciel "Berlioz", Place des Lavoirs, F-30350 Lédignan, France; tel. +33 66-83-46-53. This is a series of three programs for the Macintosh that has been written in *C* by Dominique Montel and Frédéric Magiera. *PostScript* files for output to laser printers and phototypesetters are generated. *Berlioz*, which is in use at the printing establishment s.a.r.l. Dominique Montel, is also available for licensing. Illustrated in 1990.

C-Lab Notator. See **Notator**.

Calliope. *Calliope* is a UNIX-based printing program under development by William Clocksin, Computing Laboratory, University of Cambridge, New Museums Site,

Pembroke St., Cambridge, CB2 3QG, UK; e-mail: *fennel@cl.cam.ac.uk*. A graphics-based program, *Calliope* has extensive capabilities for printing early repertories (up to 1640). Originally developed to run under *X Windows* on Sun workstations, *Calliope* is being adapted to run on the NeXT.

CCARH. CCARH, 525 Middlefield Rd., Ste. 120, Menlo Park, CA 94025; tel. (415) 322-7050; fax (415) 322-7050; e-mail: *XB.L36@Stanford.Bitnet*; *XB.L36@Forsythe. Stanford.Edu*. The Center's music representation system supports the development of electronic transcriptions and editions of a large quantity of musical repertory, chiefly from the sixteenth through the eighteenth centuries. An updated description of the *MuseData* representation scheme is available at minimal cost from CCARH. A corollary music printing system, developed by Walter B. Hewlett, has been used to produce performing scores of major works by Bach, Handel, and Telemann. Examples appear on pp. 104-5.

CMN (Common Music Notation). *CMN* is a LISP-based common music notation developed by Bill Schottstaedt, Center for Computer Research in Music and Acoustics, Stanford University, Stanford, CA 94305; tel. (415) 725-3580; e-mail: *bil@ccrma. stanford.edu*. This package available free at the anonymous FTP site *ccrma-ftp. stanford.edu* as *pub/cmn.tar.Z*. Its input is a LISP expression using various standard musical names (e.g. *c4* for Middle C, *e* for eighth-note, etc.). Its output is normally a *PostScript* program. *CMN* currently uses the Adobe *Sonata* font for clefs and other complicated symbols. It is aimed primarily at composers using Heinrich Taube's *Common Music*, and in that connection will eventually have a mouse-driven editor and other features. It can be used as a stand-alone Western music notation program, but is a bit tedious to operate in that mode. The sources for *CMN* are offered at no charge and with no restrictions on their use, but in return the developer cannot promise to provide technical support. He will make every effort, however, to correct bugs as they are reported to him.

Comus. Comus Music Printing and Publishing, Armthorpe, Tixall, Stafford ST18 0XP, England; tel. +44 0785-662520. The proprietary music printing program developed by John Dunn for this firm uses *DARMS* encoding of data and produces high resolution, device-independent graphics output. Designed originally for a UNIX environment, versions have run on a variety of machines from mainframes to an IBM PC-AT (the current host). A DOS version is now available, and the source code (in standard

[Kernighan and Ritchie] C) is also supplied on a trust basis. A previewer (VGA driver) and a graphics-based *DARMS* editor are also part of the system.

The Copyist III. Dr. T's Music Software, 124 Crescent Rd., Suite 3, Needham, MA 02194; tel. (617) 455-1454; fax (617) 455-1460. Three versions of this commercial program for Atari, Amiga, and IBM PC compatibles are offered by Dr. T's. "III" is the most comprehensive version and the one best suited to academic applications. *MIDI* input and output are supported. Files, which are edited graphically on the screen, can be converted to *Tagged Image File Format (TIFF)*, a compressed representation of graphics information, and *Encapsulated PostScript (EPS)*. Output to *PostScript* and *Ultrascript* printers as well as the Hewlett Packard LaserJet Plus and plotters is supported. *The Copyist* interfaces with a number of popular sequencer and publishing programs. The developer is Crispin Sion. Also illustrated in 1990 and preceding years.

Dai Nippon Music Processor. Dai Nippon Printing Co., Ltd., CTS Division, 1-1 Ichigaya-kagacho 1-chome, Shinjuku-ku, Tokyo 162-01, Japan; fax +81 03-3266-4199. This dedicated hardware system for the production of musical scores was announced five years ago and illustrations were provided in 1988 and 1990. Input is alphanumeric. Screen editing is supported. Output files can be sent to *MIDI* instruments, to *PostScript* printers, to a Digiset typesetter, or to the *Standard Music Expression (SMX)* file format used in music research at Waseda University. Kentaro Oka, the author of a recent article [*cf. CM 1991*, p.20] on the use of Standard Generalized Markup Language for music documents, is the current manager. Illustrated in 1991 and previous years.

Darbellay Music Processor. See **WOLFGANG**.

DARMS is an encoding system that originated in the 1960's. Various dialects have been used in several printing programs including those of A-R Editions, *The Note Processor*, *Comus*, and systems developed at the State University of New York at Binghamton by Harry Lincoln and at the University of Nottingham, England, by John Morehen. A sample of the code was shown in the *1987 Directory*, p. 12.

Dean, Jeffrey. The Stingray Office, 16 Charles Street, Oxford OX4 3AS, England; tel./fax (+44) 865-727060; e-mail: *oxcomray@vax.oxford.ac.uk*. Jeffrey Dean, a registered user of *Finale*, is a musicologist specializing in the 15th and 16th centuries who now works as a free-lance book designer and typesetter. Examples of his work, displaying the typefaces he has designed in order to reproduce all the symbols of mensural notation, can be found in forthcoming publications of Oxford University Press. Rather than make the set of typefaces available commercially, Mr. Dean hopes that scholars wishing to use them in their publications will ask him to do the typesetting. He is also considering making available bitmapped fonts so that musicologists may use the characters in low resolution.

DXF. See *Graphics file formats*.

EASY KEY. John Clifton, 175 W. 87th St., Ste. 27E, New York, NY 10024; tel. (212) 724-1578. *Easy Key* simplifies the use of Jim Miller's *Personal Composer* input and printing program.

ERATO Music Manuscriptor. See under *Music Manuscriptor*.

ESCORT. Passport Designs, 625 Miramontes Street, Half Moon Bay, CA 94019; tel. (415) 726-0280. *Escort* facilitates input from a *MIDI* device to the *SCORE* printing program.

ESTAFF. A notation program for single-voiced melodies. It automatically translates any file encoded in *ESAC* into conventional staff notation, and is compatible with the Essen *MAPPET* files (now numbering some 13,000 documented melodies). *ESTAFF* can also be used to write notes onto a blank staff, custom design musical graphics, and even convert Western notation into Chinese Jianpu notation with automatic text underlay. Other features include text, print, graphics, and playback options. Available free by license to interested researchers. For more information please contact Helmut Schaffrath at the Universität Essen, FB 4 - Musik-Postfach, W-4300 Essen 1, Germany; e-mail: *JMP100@DE0HRZ1A.BITNET*.

EUTERPE. 99 rue Frédéric Mistral, F-03100 Montluçon, France; tel. +33 70-036903. *Euterpe,* by Michel Wallet, forms part of an integrated system for encoding, printing, and analysis on the Macintosh. Special attention has been devoted to lute music and late Byzantine music. Transcription and conversion capabilities for German lute tablature to staff notation, based on programs by Bernard Stepien, were shown in 1988. The printing of Byzantine notation with text underlay in Cyrillic characters was shown in 1990.

FASTCODE.   An encoding language of the 1970's developed at Princeton University for white mensural notation.   An example of plotter output from 1981, first shown in 1985, was repeated in 1990.

Finale.   Coda Music Software, Wenger Music Learning Systems, 1401 E. 79th St., Bloomington, MN 55420-1126; technical support tel. (612) 854-9649; CompuServe 75300,3727.   *Finale* has a broad range of capabilities [itemized in *CM 1991*, p. 162] related to music transcription and printing.   Originally for the Macintosh, it is now available in a Windows/PC version as well.   *MusicProse*, a subset of *Finale* features made available at reduced cost, is reviewed by Nicholas Carter in *Computers and the Humanities* 26/1 (1992), 59-62.

Coda consistently fails to respond to enquiries from CCARH.   Jeffrey Dean shows his extensions to *Finale* for mensural notation on p. 164.

Giller, Don.   300 W. 106th St. #22, New York, NY 10025; tel. (212) 663-0515; CompuServe 71310,561.   Don Giller has been working as a free-lance music book editor and music and math desktop publisher since 1985.   The examples contributed to the present volume were mainly created using *Music Engraver* on a Macintosh II.   Giller prefers Adobe's *Sonata* font to *Music Engraver's* proprietary *Interlude* and exports each music file directly into Adobe's *Illustrator*, a *PostScript* graphics program, in which any individual component may be modified or corrected, and where components best produced by a graphics program can be added.

Graphic Notes.   See *Music Publisher*.

Graphics file formats.   The scaling of notation, the integration of musical examples in text files, and the interchange of music printing files between programs are three capabilities that depend, in many computer environments, on the ability to export notation files via a recognized graphics file format to external programs.   Many such formats are in use. Those most commonly cited by our contributors are *DXF*, which is supported by *AutoCAD*; *Encapsulated PostScript (EPS)*, which creates files for a *PostScript* printer; *HPGL*, which creates a Hewlett-Packard Graphics Language plotter file; *PC Paintbrush* format *(PCX)*; and *Tagged Image File Format (TIFF)*.

HB Music Engraver.   See *Music Engraver*.

HPGL. See *Graphics file formats*.

Humdrum *scor. See *CM 1991*, p. 67.

HyperScribe. Coda Music Software, Wenger Music Learning Systems, 1401 E. 79th St., Bloomington, MN 55420-1126; tel. (612) 854-1288. This product transcribes *MIDI* input to a Macintosh screen. It complements other products from Coda, such as *Finale*.
Interactive Music System (IMS). CERL Music Group, University of Illinois, 103 S. Mathews #252, Urbana, IL 61801-2977; tel. (217) 333-0766. This multi-faceted system has been under development at the University of Illinois, where it originated on the PLATO system, since the early 1970's. Current development is based on the Macintosh. A commercial version, *Lime* [see below], is now available for the Macintosh.

L.M.P. [Laser Music Processor] Prima. TEACH Services, 182 Donivan Rd., Brushton, NY 12916; tel. (518) 358-2125. A demo file of Version 3.2 (LMP32P.ZIP) is available on CompuServe. In this program for IBM PC compatibles note entry is by computer keyboard, mouse, standard *MIDI* file transcription, or *MIDI* device. More than 400 symbols are available. Dot-matrix printers can produce draft and high-resolution (240 dpi) output. A driver for the Hewlett Packard DeskJet is available as well as print-to-file and *PC Paintbrush (PCX)* image-file formats. Illustrated in 1991.

la mà de guido [*Guido's Hand*]. Apartat 23, E-08200, Sabadell (Barcelona), Spain; tel. +34 3-716-1350. This music printing software for IBM PC XT and AT computers uses an alphanumeric input system based on a redefined QWERTY keyboard (shown in the *1988 Directory*, p. 48). It is now being marketed as an input system for *SCORE*. The developer is Llorenç Balsach.

Lime [*Lippold's Music Editor*]. Lippold Haken, CERL Sound Group, University of Illinois, 103 S. Mathews #252, Urbana, IL 61801-2977; fax (217) 244-0793. This Macintosh version of the *Interactive Music System* (see above) music printing program was developed at the University of Illinois by Haken and at Queen's University (Kingston, Ontario) by Dorothea Blostein. The current version does not generate *PostScript* files because licensing fees would approximately double the cost of the product. For information on obtaining a free demonstration copy of *Lime* by FTP over Internet, send electronic mail to *L-Haken@uiuc.edu*. A description of *Lime*'s music representation is also available to the public. Illustrated in 1991.

Mosaic. The latest notation program for the Macintosh from Mark of the Unicorn is said to handle complex meters, beam tilt, and cross-staff beaming, but no proof by way of a contribution to *CM* has been received. *Mosaic* does not recognize files from the company's well established *Professional Composer* program [see that listing for the address].

MuTeX [also **MusicTeX**] is a set of fonts, developed by Angelika Schofer and Andrea Steinbach, for music typesetting with the TeX document description language. The fonts and numerous printer drivers are available by FTP at several sites. Queries may be directed to Werner Icking, Gesellschaft für Mathematik und Datenverarbeitung mbH, Schloss Birlinghoven, PO Box 1316, D-5205 Sankt Augustin, Germany; tel. +49 2241/14-2443; e-mail: *icking@gmd.de*. See also pp. 47 and 53.

MusE (formerly *A-R Music Engraver*). A-R Editions, Inc., 801 Deming Way, Madison, WI 53717; tel. (608) 836-9000; fax (608) 831-8200. A commercial version of the music typesetting system used by this publisher for its own editions and musical examples for academic journals has been developed for professional music publishing and is now available by license. Tom Hall is the principal developer. This version of the program, for the UNIX operating system, uses the *OpenWindows* interface on the Sun SPARC and SPARC-compatible workstations with a high resolution monitor (1600 x 1280). Music input is done alphanumerically with a modified version of *DARMS*; files may be created on other systems before processing and editing on the workstation. *PostScript* images may be imported to the music page, and likewise, *MusE* can create *EPS* graphics files for export into other programs.

A music notation library developed by A-R and multiple text fonts created by Mergenthaler are cross-licensed and available for use with the program. *PostScript* printers and typesetters are supported.

Music Engraver (formerly **HB Music Engraver**). Ken Johnson, Music Engraver, 7725 E. 14th Ave., Denver, CO 80220; tel. (303) 329-6468. This printing program runs on the Apple Macintosh and produces output for *PostScript* printers. Input is alphanumeric and utilizes redefinition of the QWERTY keyboard. No direct contribution has been received in recent years. For examples of what the program can do, see the contributions of Don Giller in 1991 and 1992.

Music Manuscriptor. Erato Software Corp., PO Box 6278, Salt Lake City, UT 84152-6278; tel. (801) 328-0500. This commercially available program operates as part of an integrated workstation for composition and orchestration. Setup requires an IBM PC compatible microcomputer, a digitizer tablet or mouse, *MIDI* device, math chip, and laser printer (HP or Canon). Super-VGA and large format displays up to 2400 x 1600 pixels are available. Pitches are entered and edited as *MIDI* data; other commands and controls are keyed in from the tablet. 1000 slots of clipboard storage is provided for repeated passages or motifs. Output is to *TIFF* files. Print output comes in four standard engraving sizes. There is also 32-channel audio playback and an early music feature.

The *Music Manuscriptor* is currently being used by *MusicText* in London to typeset a complete critical performing edition of the madrigals of Monteverdi. In the US, the system is in use for several films; completed files are transferred to workstations at Twentieth Century Fox for part extraction and printing.

Music Publisher. Repertoire Pty. Ltd., 49A Stephens Terrace, St. Peters, South Australia 5069, Australia; tel. +61 8/363-2600; fax +61 8/363-2610. The product has recently been distributed in the US by InterSoft of Soquel, CA 95062; tel. (408) 476-2674. This program, developed by Trevor Richards for the Apple Macintosh, requires the use of a separate "presto pad" for input. It provides output for *PostScript* printers and typesetters. Examples were shown in 1988. No contribution has been provided since.

MusicEase. Grandmaster, Inc., PO Box 2567, Spokane, WA 99220-2567; tel. (509) 747-6773. This commercial product for IBM PC compatibles is primarily intended for on-screen assembly and editing of musical data, but it can also accept *MIDI* data in real time or step time. *MIDI* files may be imported and exported. Illustrated in 1991.

MusicPrinter Plus. Temporal Acuity Products, Inc., 300 120th Avenue N.E., Bldg. 1, Bellevue, WA 98005; tel. (800) 426-2673. CompuServe offers a demo of Version 3.2 (MPPLUS.ZIP) and a features list for Version 4.1 (MPP41.TXT). TAP is a noted manufacturer of interactive systems for rhythmic drill and other music teaching products. Its music printing program, originally designed by Jack Jarrett, is for MS DOS machines. Version 4.0, which is *MIDI* compatible, permits double-staff input. The playback choices include real time and step time, which can be forward or backward; much subtlety of articulation is supported. Dot matrix, laser, and ink jet printers are supported. Wide-carriage output on the BJ-130 provides 360 dpi resolution. A submission was last received in 1989.

MusicProse. See *Finale*.

Musicwriter II. See *The Portable Musicwriter*.

MusiKrafters. MusiKrafters, PO Box 14124, Louisville, KY 40214; tel. (502) 361-4597. This software company offers special-purpose products by Robert Fruehwald for musical excerpts and unusual notations for the Apple Macintosh. Input is alphanumeric and may be edited on the screen. *PostScript* files are produced. Its shape-note and tablature capabilities were shown in 1988 and a *HyperText* program for musical information management was shown in 1989.

MusScribe. See *NoteWriter*.

MUZIKA. *MUZIKA* is a object-oriented notation program for the PC. It is being developed in Israel using Borland's *C++*. It is designed to run under *Windows 3.0*, relies on screen assembly using a mouse, and provides *MIDI* output. At present it provides only screen display of notation. It is intended to facilitate creation of scores and editing of parts. It is available by FTP [from *piano.technion.ac.il* / 132.68.48.181] in three parts: a user's guide is in *muzpak.txt;* source files and documentation are in *muzsrc.zip*; *muzpak.zip* is an executable file.

Nightingale. Advanced Music Notation Systems, PO Box 60356, Florence, MA 01060; tel. (413) 586-3958; e-mail: *don@cogsci.indiana.edu*. Don Byrd's Macintosh program for music notation will be made available by Temporal Acuity Products, Inc., 300 120th Avenue N.E., Bldg. 1, Bellevue, WA 98005; tel. (800) 426-2673. *Nightingale* uses *MIDI* input. Output may be edited graphically and further revised in popular desktop publishing programs.

This year's contribution was produced by beta-tester John Gibson. Gibson is an independent engraver who uses *Nightingale* in contract work. He may be reached at 44 Vandevanter Ave. #3, Princeton, NJ 08540; tel. (609) 921-8905; e-mail: *gibson@silvertone.edu*. The program has also been tested extensively with both early and contemporary repertories by Tim Crawford at King's College in the University of London.

Notator. C-Lab Software GmbH, Postfach 700303, D-2000 Hamburg 70, Germany; tel. +49 040-694400-0. Now distributed in the US by Ensonix Corp., 155 Great Valley

Parkway, Malvern, PA 19355; tel. (215) 647-3930. The design intent behind this software package by Gerhard Lengeling and Chris Adam for the Atari ST series was to combine advanced sequencing and notational capabilities in one product. As such, it stresses flexibility of input (primarily *MIDI*), editing control, efficient performance-to-printed-page interface, and overall ease of use. For those chiefly interested in notation, a junior version called *Alpha* is available, with the main difference being in the sequencer. Illustrated in 1991. A companion product, *Aura*, is an interactive program for music theory and ear training.

The Note Processor. Thoughtprocessors, 584 Bergen Street, Brooklyn, NY 11238; tel. (718) 857-2860; fax (718) 398-8411; CompuServe: 73700,3475. A demo (NOTEPR.ZIP) and guitar fonts (NPGUI.ZIP) are available on CompuServe. Stephen Dydo's program for IBM PC compatibles accepts both alphanumeric and *MIDI* input; data can be edited either through code revisions or on screen with a mouse. The input code is a dialect of *DARMS*. Numerous dot matrix printers as well as the Hewlett Packard DeskJet and LaserJet printers are supported. *MIDI* output and file interchange with sequencer programs are supported. The optional *Engraver's Font Set* enables users to create their own symbols; the optional *Outline Option* produces *PostScript* files.

NoteWriter II. Passport Designs, 625 Miramontes, Half Moon Bay, CA 94019; tel. (415) 726-0280. This commercial product for the Apple Macintosh is the heir of *MusScribe* (shown in 1988) and has been developed by Keith Hamel of Richmond, BC, Canada. *NoteWriter*, which is *PostScript* compatible, is used to typeset musical examples in several scholarly and popular music journals. *QuickScrawl* mode permits users to draw freehand. Analytical examples submitted by a user, John William Schaffer, were shown in 1991.

Oberon Music Editor. Oberon Systems, PO Box 4179, Boulder, CO 80306-4179; tel. (303) 459-3411. This program for IBM PC compatibles is available as a stand-alone product or on a license basis. Entry is alphanumeric and supports printing only. A custom font, *Callisto*, and a multi-size font set called *Publisher Series* are available. A shape-note version of the editor is also available. Musical examples can be integrated with *WordPerfect* files and output to *PostScript* printers. Compatibility with *Ventura Publisher* is currently being implemented.

PCX. See *Graphics file formats*.

Personal Composer. David Moore, Softelligence, 3213 W. Wheeler St., Ste. 140, Seattle, WA 98199; tel. (206) 546-4800; fax (206) 284-3898. CompuServe provides a demo (PCMPDE.ZIP). Technical support is available by telephone at (206) 236-0105. This program by Jim Miller for the IBM PC line accepts *MIDI* and alphanumeric input and outputs *PostScript* files. See also *Easy Key*.

Philip's Music Scribe (PMS). 33 Metcalfe Road, Cambridge CB4 2DB, England; tel. +44 223-334714; e-mail: *ph10@cus.cam.ac.uk*. This program by Philip Hazel for the Acorn Archimedes computer uses alphanumeric input and produces *PostScript* files as its `top quality' output, though several other printers are supported. It runs on Acorn's proprietary RISC operating system. Acorn products are currently available in the UK, Europe, Australia, New Zealand, and South Africa.

PMS, which is now commercially available, has extensive capabilities for accommodating the needs of parts and scores derived from a common input file. Staves can be overlaid, permitting four-part choral music to be shown on two staves, for example. Up to four verses of text underlay can be accommodated. Slur control is extensive. Basso continuo figuration is supported. Time signatures can be switched off. All characters found in the *PMS* music font set are also available for use in text strings.

Plaine and Easie. This melodic input code developed by Barry Brook and Murray Gould in the late 1960's remains important because of its extensive use in thematic indexing projects, especially the manuscript cataloguing effort of the International Inventory of Musical Sources (RISM) coordinated in Frankfurt, Germany. Diverse printing programs for RISM data have been written. Output from one by Norbert Böker-Heil was shown in the *1988 Directory*, p. 19. A program for data verification by Brent Field has been in active use for the last few years. Documentation is available from RISM Zentralredaktion, Sopienstr. 26, W-6000 Frankfurt-am-Main 90, Germany, and John Howard, Music Library, Harvard University, Cambridge, MA 02138; e-mail: *howard@harvarda*.

PLAINSONG. Royal Holloway and Bedford New College (Computer Centre, Egham Hill, Egham, Surrey TW20 0EX, England; e-mail: *C.Harbor@vax.rhbnc.ac.uk*). *PLAINSONG* is a series of programs for transcription, analysis, and printing of music in black square neumatic notation on a four-line stave with C, F, D, or G clefs. It is under development by Catherine Harbor and Andy Reid. *PLAINSONG* runs on the IBM PC. Dot matrix and *PostScript* laser printers may be used. The work is described in

Catherine Harbor, "*PLAINSONG*—A Program for the Study of Chant in Neumatic Notation," *Computers in Music Research Conference Handbook* (Belfast: The Queen's University, 1991), pp. 24-5.

The Portable Musicwriter. Music Print Corp., 2620 Lafayette Drive, Boulder, CO 80303; tel. (303) 499-2552. This method for printing musical examples, developed by Cecil Effinger, a recognized pioneer in music printing technology, requires an IBM Wheelwriter. The resolution is 104 dpi vertically and 120 dpi horizontally. Music is represented alphanumerically. Slurs are added by hand. Shown in 1990 and previous years.

Professional Composer. Mark of the Unicorn, 222 Third St., Cambridge, MA 02142; tel. (617) 576-2760. This commercial product for the Apple Macintosh has been poorly represented in previous years because of its failure to provide any material other than advertising copy. A third-party contribution appears on pp. 108-9.

SCORE. US sales and support: 3732 Laguna St., Palo Alto, CA 94306; tel./fax (415) 853-9394. A demo (SCORE.ARC) is available on CompuServe. Overseas sales continue to be handled by Passport Designs [see next entry]. Leland Smith's *SCORE* program for IBM PC compatibles is now in use by many major music publishers. Translation programs to and from the *SCORE* format are also beginning to appear. The original input system is alphanumeric and requires separate passes for pitch, rhythm, and articulation. Several supplementary products provide other means of input [*cf. Escort, la mà de guido,* and *ScoreInput*]. Forty music fonts are available. There is a *PostScript* text font compatibility.

ScoreInput. Passport Designs, 625 Miramontes Street, Half Moon Bay, CA 94019; tel. (415) 726-0280. *ScoreInput* is a program by Paul Nahay to generate input for Leland Smith's *SCORE* program either from a *MIDI* keyboard or through redefinition of a QWERTY keyboard. The developer claims that it is faster and more accurate than other front ends for *SCORE*.

SCRIBE. Scribe Software Associates, La Trobe University, Bundoora, Victoria 3083, Australia; tel. +61 03-479-2879. User support is available by fax +61 03-478-5814 and e-mail: *MUSJS@lure.latrobe.edu.au*. This academic research system developed jointly by La Trobe and Melbourne Universities for fourteenth-century music is oriented mainly toward database management of musical repertories. The program is available by license to both individuals and institutional sites and runs on IBM PC compatibles. The original software has been developed by John Griffiths and Brian Parish. John Stinson is the head musicologist.

Subtilior Press. 292 Maurice Street, London, Ontario N6H 1C5, Canada; tel. (519) 642-4510. David Palmer's *Subtilior Press* is a program for late-Medieval and Renaissance mensural notation that runs on a Macintosh Plus with *HyperCard*. Transcriptions are assembled on the screen from graphic elements. The price is extremely modest. Examples including illuminated initials, ligatures, and white mensural notation were shown in 1989.

Synclavier Music Engraving System. New England Digital Corp., 85 Mechanic St., Lebanon, NH 03766; tel. (603) 448-5870; fax (603) 448-3684. The *Synclavier Music Engraving System* is offered by New England Digital both as a stand-alone workstation and as an adjunct to their larger audio and music processing systems. Several less common notations, including shape notes and guitar tablature, are supported. *PostScript* files are produced. Gregg Sewell, an engraver at 518 N. Cherry St., Florence, AL 35630; tel. (205) 764-6212, has engraved examples for recent issues of this publication. Alan Talbot serves as an independent consultant on printing applications of the system and has coordinated all submissions representing this system. Illustrated in 1991 and previous years.

TELETAU. Pisa and Florence, Italy. *TELETAU* is an integrated system for musical data management initially developed at CNUCE in Pisa; it is now maintained jointly with the Florence Conservatory.

THEME, The Music Editor. THEME Music Software, PO Box 8204, Charlottesville, VA 22906; tel. (804) 971-5963. A demo (THDEMO.ZIP) and several printing samples are available on CompuServe. This commercial product, developed by Mark Lambert for the IBM PC, has been used extensively in academic settings. Its alphanumeric input system uses a redefined keyboard (shown in 1988). It has a provision for *MIDI* input and for conversion of alphanumeric files to *MIDI* output. Optimization of page layout is automatic. Binary-encoded data sets are available to users. Output was last provided in 1989.

TIFF. See *Graphics file formats*.

Toppan Scan-Note System. Toppan International Group, Iwanami Shoten Annex Bldg. 2-3-1, Kanda Jimbocho, Chiyoda-ku, Tokyo 101, Japan. The Toppan system originated in Aarhus, Denmark, where it was developed by Mogens Kjaer. It is at present a proprietary system that accepts electronic keyboard input and prints music with a laser phototypesetter. Toppan Printing Co. Ltd. contracts with major music publishers and has produced some recent volumes of the *Neue Mozart Ausgabe*. Illustrations were shown in 1987.

Virtuoso. Musical notation represents one capability of this interactive music system under development for the Macintosh and PCs running *Windows*. An expert system provides the foundation for the product, which will be available toward the end of 1992 from Virtuoso Software, Inc., 742 Dudley Avenue, Winnipeg, Manitoba, Canada R3M 1S1; tel. (204) 452-0508.

WOLFGANG. Société Mus'Art, Case Postale 26, CH-1242 Satigny, Geneva, Switzerland. A demo (WOLFGA.LZH) is available on CompuServe. This academically oriented music processor, developed by Etienne Darbellay for IBM PC compatibles, was awarded the Swiss Prize for Technology for 1990. The keyboard is fully user-definable. Screen resolutions to 1664 x 1200 are supported. Files can be converted to *TIFF* compressed or uncompressed formats and used with such desktop publishing programs as *Ventura Publisher* and *Aldus Pagemaker*. An interface with the ADLIB sound driver exists.

WOLFGANG has the ability to represent and reproduce plainchant, mensural notation (black and white, ligatures), and the unmeasured *style brisé*. It also supports automatic reduction to a two-stave transcription of up to five voices and permits the creation of polylingual scores requiring Arabic, Cyrillic, and Gothic (as well as Roman) characters. Output was shown in 1990.

The Musical Notation Quiz:
Responses and New Questions

In the 1991 edition of *CM*, software developer Don Byrd (Advanced Music Notation Systems, P.O. Box 60356, Florence, MA 01060) offered a series of eighteen questions about extremes of musical notation. Software developers are interested in defining these extremes because they want to be sure that their products can accommodate them. Byrd, the author of *Nightingale*, has been actively involved in the development of music printing software for 20 years.

While our annual gallery of musical notation samples always demonstrates capabilities in areas recognized for their inherent difficulty, we have not in general probed the extremes to which that Byrd's quiz points. This is because the problem areas we choose for our set examples are commonly encountered in performing and scholarly editions, while some of the examples cited here may pass the majority of musicians and music scholars unnoticed. Software support for these rare cases is achievable, sometimes almost instantaneously—once the need has been specified. As several readers pointed out, *Finale* can handle 4096th notes. All it needs is some music to try them out on.

* * *

We promised a complete run of *CM* to the person who could provide answers to the largest number of questions. The hands-down winner was pianist, conductor, and author Mark Starr, whose knowledge of nineteenth-century French music seems to have been a special asset in this undertaking. Determining a second-place winner was a tougher call. We have designated music theorist Stan Shumway, whose responses appear first, the official runner-up.

We fully intended to allow our readers a year in which to submit responses to a new set of questions posed by Starr, but the curious career of the composer Alkan, who figures in the answers to two of them as well as to one of Byrd's questions, so engaged our interest that we decided to run the answers and supporting documentation together with Starr's questions. This enables us to append two questions posed by Nigel Nettheim (a free copy of the 1992 and 1993 issues of *CM* is promised for the most complete response to his questions).

The editors express their special gratitude to Don Byrd, whose second list of questions will appear in 1993, and to the other respondents.

Responses to Don Byrd's Quiz

From Stan Shumway, Professor of Music Theory, The University of Kansas, Department of Music and Dance, School of Fine Arts, Lawrence, KS 66045-2279:

The American composer Anthony Philip Heinrich (1781-1861) used 1024th notes, and even two 2048th notes, in his *Toccata Grande Cromatica* for piano (see J. Bunker Clark, *The Dawning of American Keyboard Music,* Greenwood Press, 1988, p. 365).

Kaikhosru Sorabji, real name Leon Dudley, b. 1892, wrote a piece called *Opus Clavicembalisticum* in 1930, taking about five hours to perform. It is in three parts with 12 subdivisions, including a theme with 49 variations and a passacaglia with 81 variations. A piece by the American composer John Powell, recorded by Roy Hamlin Johnson, entitled *Sonata Teutonica* is exceptionally long.

From Mark Starr, 123 Loucks Avenue, Los Altos, CA 94022:

Longest movement in measures? The *Etude No. 8 en Sol dièse mineur* from the *Douze études dans tous les tons mineurs,* Opus 39, by the 19th century French composer Charles-Valentin Alkan, at 1345 bars in 3/4, is surely much longer than the *Finale* of Schubert's Symphony No. 9 (1154 bars in 2/4) [Byrd's provisional answer]. Alkan's *Etude No. 8* is one of three movements (the other two are the *Etude No. 9 en Do dièse mineur* and the *Etude No. 10 en Fa dièse mineur*) that constitute his monumental *Concerto* of 1857 for piano alone.

Longest movement in time? In 1978, in a series of conversations on KQED-FM [San Francisco], the legendary Hungarian pianist Ervin Nyreghazi confided to me that he had composed more than one thousand works throughout his life. He said that one of them, an orchestral tone poem in one movement entitled "The Picture of Dorian Gray" after the famous story by Oscar Wilde, would take "about three or four hours to perform." But he added that he couldn't be sure of the duration, since the work had never been performed; it might actually take much longer.

The scene from Goethe's *Faust* in Mahler's Symphony No. 8 is probably the longest published continuous movement. Because of the enormous forces involved, it is probably also the movement with the largest number of written notes. (*You* can count them!) Schoenberg's *Gurrelieder* might also qualify for these distinctions, although that work can hardly be called a continuous movement (it is more like a cantata or a concert opera). However, the award for the published work for one player with the most notes and the longest duration probably goes to Kaikhosru Sorabji's *Opus Clavicembalisticum*, for piano.

Most ledger lines below the staff? Several composers have used six ledger lines for A0 on the piano. The first, however, was Alkan, in his published cadenzas of 1860 for Mozart's Piano Concerto in D Minor.

Lowest sounding pitch? The Bösendorfer *Imperiale* concert grand piano has a compartment that opens, revealing keys that go down to C0. These notes are usually used to continue octave passages by virtuoso piano composers like Liszt and Busoni, who run out of notes below A0. (When one first sits down with the full keyboard exposed, it is hard to find Middle C). I have never seen a C0 in print. But since the note exists not only on the Bösendorfer but also on the *MIDI* scale, it might be wise for developers to include it in their programs.

Longest notated duration, including ties? The longest note ever notated in a published score may be that in Act I of Verdi's *Otello*. The opera opens with a cluster in the organ, notated in three whole notes *C2*, *C#2*, and *D2*, sounding (according to Verdi's written instructions) *C1*, *C#1*, and *D1*. This cluster of three notes is sustained for 256 bars of 4/4 (it is written out with ties). When the note cluster is released (at rehearsal letter T in my score), the chorus says "Si calma la bufera," and Verdi tells the organist he can go home.

Highest sounding pitch? The selection of the *C#8* in Schoenberg's Violin Concerto struck me as an end run, since it is an artificial harmonic. For a real note, how about the *B6* sounding *B7* in the piccolo part of *Antiphysis* by Hugues Dufourt?

Regarding Tchaikovsky's six **p**'s for the bassoon solo in the first movement of the *Pathétique,* most conductors substitute a bass clarinet—since bassoons often crack when played very, very, very, very, very, very softly. But Tchaikovsky was not the only composer to use six **p**'s. Look in bar 37 of the duet for Otello and Desdemona in Act 1 of Verdi's *Otello*. Of course, quieter still is John Cage's piano piece 4'33" (unless you count the audience noise).

Most notes in a vertical simultaneity? Charles Ives, *Three Places in New England,* third movement (from "The Housatonic at Stockbridge"). At letter J, the piano part contains a chord with 16 notes in the treble clef and 18 notes in the bass clef. On the following 32nd note, seven more notes are added to the chord, for a grand total of 40 notes sounding virtually simultaneously. Needless to say, the piano part is usually tackled by two orchestral pianists when it is performed. This chord would also qualify for *The Most Notes on a Single Stem* award—except for the fact that these notes are whole notes, with no stems.

"The Housatonic at Stockbridge" also deserves the prize for *Most Complex Tuplet.* Almost any bar from the first violin part will do, for the simple reason that after the first note, very few of the many complex tuplets ever fall on a beat, or even on a simple division of a beat. Consequently, like irrational numbers, the beats cannot be subdivided. As written, these rhythms are uncountable. Indeed, in the published orchestral materials of this work, the first violin part has been renotated into approximations of Ives's tuplets, but here the tuplets fall on beats.

Nigel Nettheim, 204A Beecroft Road, Cheltenham, NSW 2119, Australia, brings a different perspective to the longest movement question:

...it has a bearing on the attention span of human beings. Roughly speaking the maximum attention span is about twenty minutes, and this also apparently applies to the time a chess-player can profitably study a position. If he exceeds this, he may well become confused and wish he'd called a halt earlier, or taken a break analogous to the break between movements. In the case of minimalist music some unbroken performances have, I believe, gone on for some days, but they do not require concentration in the usual sense.

Mark Starr's Quiz [answers on the next page]

1. The only published work that employs triple sharps? (Incidentally, their usage is harmonically correct.)

2. Name a published work in which none of the staffs is parallel to any other staff. (Exclude the circular staffs of George Crumb and others.)

3. Name a published orchestral work in which an instrument plays exactly one note in each of the work's three movements.

4. Name at least three published pieces in which a pitch is repeated from beginning to end.

5. The most grace notes on one beam?

6. The longest tempo indication?

7. Lowest note ever written for the oboe?

Nigel Nettheim's Questions
[Answers please to 204A Beecroft Road, Cheltenham, NSW 2119, Australia, by March 31, 1992]

Two questions of some interest to me as a programmer are:

1. What is the maximum number of notes in a bar?

2. What is the maximum number of notes in one "voice" in a bar? (Perhaps encountered in one of Chopin's florid passages?)

Mark Starr's Provisional Answers

1. Alkan, Etude No. 10, from the *Douze études dans tous les tons mineurs*, Opus 39; bars 246 and 291. [See the example on p. 190. The vertical indications and other features of the notation are also of interest.]

2. Sylvano Bussotti, *ancora odono i colli.*

3. Honegger, Symphony No. 5 (*Di tre re*). The solo timpani plays one D for the last note of each movement.

4. (a) Alkan, *Fa.*
   (b) Ravel, *Gaspard de la nuit* (second movement).
   (c) Madrigal written by Roland de Lassus with a vocal part on one note for the king to sing.

5. 28 grace notes on one beam in the solo flute part of *Antiphysis* by Hugues Dufourt.

6. From the *Kyrie* of Beethoven's Mass in C, Opus 86:   *Andante con moto assai vivace, quasi Allegretto, ma non troppo.*

7. *A3*; John Corigliano, Concerto for Oboe and Orchestra.

...and a Note from the Editors

Steve Rasmussen of CCARH explored the reference to the madrigal in answer #4c and reports that the work in question was (spuriously) attributed not to Lassus but to Josquin; the actual author is unknown.

The musical work, which is the equivalent of 50 bars in 4/4, seems to originate with the title "Guillaume se va chaufer." It was Glareanus, whose version from the *Dodecachordon* of 1547 we reproduce below, who was responsible for the legend that the work was written to accommodate the singing abilities of King Louis XIII. Accordingly, he identified it as "Lutuichi Regis Franciae jocosa cantio."

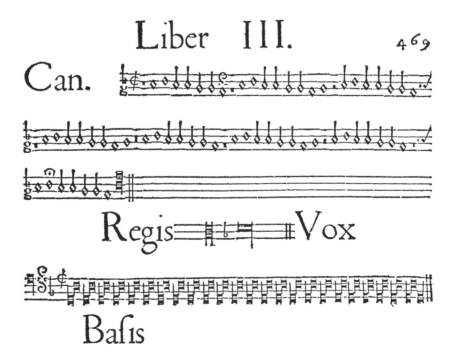

Anonymous madrigal for King Louis XIII to sing.

Anyone who thought that the excerpt from Ravel's *Gaspard de la nuit* sent to software developers in 1991 was peerless in its demands need only turn to the following excerpt from the Alkan *Etude* No. 10 [from *Douze études dans tous les tons mineurs*, Op. 39] for enlightenment.

Alkan: *Etude* **Op. 39, No. 10, in F# Minor (excerpt).**
Note the triple sharp in the left-hand part of the second bar shown.

Current Chronicle

Current Chronicle
Conferences

Cognitive Musicology: Jyvaeskylae

The First International Conference on Cognitive Musicology will be held at the University of Jyvaeskylae, Finland, from August 26 to 29, 1993. Notices of interest may be sent until February 15, 1993, to Jukka Louhivouri, University of Jyvae-skylae, Department of Musicology, PL 35, 40351 Jyvaeskylae, Finland; tel. +358 41/601 337; fax +358 41/601 331; e-mail: *louhivou@tukki.jyu.fi.* The language of the conference is English. The proceedings will be published at the start of the conference.

Topics to be emphasized include knowledge representation, artificial musical intelligence, reason and affect, neurophysiological research; pedagogy, theory, analysis, composition, performance, and historical studies; semiotics and hermeneutics; and digital technology. Members of the program committee are Antonio Camurri, Otto Laske, Marc Leman, Jukka Louhivuori, and Alan Marsden.

ECAI: Vienna

This year's conference on Artificial Intelligence and Music, on August 3 and 4, at the University of Vienna was organized by Gerhard Widmer on the general theme of "Representation of Musical Knowledge." Speakers and topics were to have included two presentations with a music-theoretical component by Ozgur

Izmirli and Semih Bilgen (Ankara; "Classification of Note-Rhythm Complexities in Melodies Using a Neural Network Model") and Klaus Balzer (Berlin; "Counterpoint and Geometry") as well as papers by Petri Toiviainen (Jyvaeskylae, Finland), Ioannis Zannos (Tokyo), Francis Courtot (Paris), Marc Leman (Ghent) and Neil P. McA. Todd (London) relating to perception, acoustics, and their representation.

In addition, Antonio Camurri (Genoa) chaired a panel on "Analogical and Symbolic Representations of Musical Knowledge." Further details are available from the organizer at the Austrian Research Institute for Artificial Intelligence, Schottengasse 3, A-1010 Vienna, Austria; tel. +43 222/53532810; fax +43 222/ 630652; e-mail: *gerhard@ai.univie. ac.at.*

ICTM Study Group on Computer Applications: Vienna

The fifth annual meeting of the International Council for Traditional Music Study Group on Computer Applications met in Vienna from September 28 to October 2, 1992. The event was hosted by the Institut für Musikwissenschaft der Universität Wien, Universitätsstr. 7, A-1010 Vienna, Austria. The meeting was organized by Emil H. Lubej. Papers and software demonstrations emphasized two principal topics—"Digital Signal Processing in Ethnomusicology: Methods and Applications" [on which see pp. 96-8] and "Representation and Analysis of Music." Software demonstrations were offered on an IBM PC compatible, an Atari, a Macintosh, and an IBM-mainframe 3090. Enquiries may be sent to Dr. Lubej by e-mail: *A7321DAC@AWIUNI11.BITNET*.

IMS Study Group: Madrid

The International Musicological Society Study Group on Musical Data and Computer Applications conducted a study session and hosted a software exhibit at the Fourteenth Congress of the Society, which was held in Madrid from April 3 to 10, 1992. The study session, "New Methodologies in the Study of Melody," included talks on segmentation, grouping, and rhythm by Moisei Boroda and Lelio Camilleri and on melodic comparison by John Stinson [early monophonic repertories], Helmut Schaffrath [folk repertories], John Howard [seventeenth- and eighteenth-century European music], and Tim Crawford [lute transcriptions]. The proceedings are currently in course of preparation. Crawford's work formed the subject of an article in the June 6, 1992, issue of the British weekly *New Scientist*.

Twelve programs for the management of musical and textual data on the MS DOS and Macintosh platforms were available for demonstration in the software exhibit, which was supervised by Helmut Schaffrath and Arvid Vollsnes. Software contributors included Eva Ferková, Helmut Schaffrath, Lelio Camilleri, Leeman Perkins, Thomas Griffin, Klaus

Keil, John Stinson, Max Haas, David Cope, David Evan Jones, David Palmer, Tim Crawford, and Tom Mathiesen.

European Conference on Music Analysis: Trent

The Second European Conference on Music Analysis took place in Trent from October 24 to 27, 1991. The event was sponsored by GATM (Italian Group on Theory and Analysis), the University of Trent, and the Accademia Filarmonica of Trent; it was organized by Rossana Dalmonte and Mario Baroni. Plenary sessions were concerned with music performance and the analysis of analysis. Roundtable subjects ranged from the analysis of modal repertories to popular music. Two demonstration periods for analytical software were scheduled.

The first demonstration session included a program for paradigmatic analysis by Lelio Camilleri, David Bencini, and Michele Ignelzi; a description of the analytical software developed in Essen by Helmut Schaffrath and his associates; and *CMAP*, a Macintosh program for pc-set analysis by Peter Castine [on the last two, see *CM 1991*, pp. 30-2 and 73-5]. In the other session, Baroni, Dalmonte, and Carlo Jacoboni illustrated the latest application of their musical grammar methodology to the repertoire of Legrenzi's cantatas. Also shown were programs for analytical usage of a system for spectral analysis and for tonal harmonic analysis (the latter by Eva Ferková; cf. pp. 85-9).

A session on the theme "Analyzing Electro-acoustic Music" was given for possibly the first time. It included papers by Denis Smalley, François Delalande, Christiane Ten Hoppen, Simonetta Sargenti, and Francesco Giomi and Marco Ligabue, each employing a different method to analyze the electro-acoustic piece *Aquatisme* by Bernard Parmegiani.

—*Lelio Camilleri*

Musical Material for and by the Blind: Tirrenia

The final EEC-sponsored workshop on the computer-aided production of music materials for and by the visually impaired took place in Tirrenia, near Pisa, on November 20 and 21, 1991. The purpose of the workshop was to show results of projects supported through the European Initiative for Technology for the Visually Impaired, which commenced in Toulouse in 1988.

Demonstrations included experimental programs and applications of commercial software, sometimes requiring additional devices, for the blind. One example of the latter kind was Paolo Razzuoli's use of the musical notation program *SCORE*. A voice synthesizer repeats all the commands he enters on the computer keyboard.

Two major projects involving the creation of Braille music output were presented. In the project supervised by Mark Glover (Royal National Institute for the Blind, UK), the *SCORE* parametric code is converted to a representation which produces Braille notation. In the work of Nadine Baptiste and Monique Truquet

(Paul Sabatier University, Toulouse), an input system involving the use of a structured alphanumeric code and a graphic editor allows the user to enter a score to be printed subsequently in Braille. In addition, an experimental version of the *Teletau* system for the PC was presented by Lelio Camilleri, Paolo Graziani, and Francesco Giomi (Divisione Musicologica CNUCE, IROE).

Another theme treated in the workshop was the acquisition of a musical score through optical recognition (OCR). A paper by R. Randriamaheta (of the Institut National des Jeunes Aveugles, Paris) described initial efforts in this area.

—*Lelio Camilleri*

Music Perception and Cognition: Los Angeles

The second International Conference on Music Perception and Cognition, held at the University of California, Los Angeles, from February 22 to 26, 1992, offered four sessions on tonal structures, three on computational models, two on neuropsychology, and many on other topics. Daniel Hersh-man (University of Washington) described experimental work indicating that rhythmic grouping factors are significant determinants of tonal recognition. Jaydeep Chakraborty (Nomura Research Institute, New York) spoke on machine recognition of ragas—a relatively stable repertory of melodic patterns each of which connotes a different mood or meaning—in Indian classical music. Since ragas are subjected to successively more elaborate improvisations in performance, their defining tones can be difficult to detect auditorily. Stewart Hulse (Dept. of Psychology, Johns Hopkins University, Baltimore) demonstrated that "melodic" recognition in starlings is inseparable from the specific timbre and tonality of the items in the learning set; the "learned" melodies are not recognized when their timbre or tonality is altered.

The next conference of the Society for Music Perception and Cognition will be held at the University of Pennsylvania in February 1993. Further information is available from Eugene Narmour, Chairman, Dept. of Music, University of Pennsylvania, 201 S. 34th St., Philadelphia, PA 19104. The 1994 event will be held in Liège, Belgium.

Music Representation: Stanford

Music Publishing and Music Representation in the Technological Age was the title of a two-day symposium held at Stanford University on January 18 and 19, 1992. Sessions on the first day concerning representation (1) for computer-interactive performance and (2) for diverse applications contrasted with more practical sessions on the second exploring (3) databases of musical information and (4) practical advantages and disadvantages of computer-generated typography.

Among the speakers were Max V. Mathews (Center for Computer Research in Music and Acoustics, Stanford), Barry Vercoe (M.I.T. Media Lab), and Jean-

Claude Risset (C.N.R.S., Marseilles) (Session 1); Nicholas Carter (University of Surrey), Miller Puckette (IRCAM, Paris), and Garrett Bowles (University of California, San Diego) (2); Leland Smith (Stanford), Walter Hewlett (Center for Computer Assisted Research in the Humanities), Steven Newcomb (Florida State University), and David Cope (University of California, Santa Cruz) (3); and Johannes Göbel (for B. Schotts Söhne, Mainz) and Andrew Potter (for Oxford University Press) (4). Those interested in the proceedings should contact Leland Smith or Patte Wood at CCRMA, Stanford University, the Knoll, Stanford, CA 94305; e-mail: *patte@ccrma.stanford.edu*.

Statistical Applications: Sydney

Nigel Nettheim has organized a session on "Computer/Statistical Applications in Music Analysis" for the National Conference of the Musicological Society of Australia. The meeting was scheduled to take place in Sydney from October 7 to 11, 1992. The provisional program listed talks by H. V. Sahasrabuddhe (Pune, India), Judith Fisher (Sydney), Glynn Marillier (Edith Cowan University, Western Australia), and Dr. Nettheim. Details may be obtained from the organizer at 204A Beecroft Road, Cheltenham, NSW 2119, Australia; tel. +61 2/868-4005; fax: +61 2/313-7682; e-mail: *nigel@cumulus.csd.unsw.oz.au*.

Electronic Conferences and Resources

[See also Using Networks], pp. 31-60]

HUMBUL

Stuart Lee is now the editor of HUMBUL, a British super-bulletin of academic news. HUMBUL provides many valuable services as well as archiving other electronic publications, including the *Music Research Digest*. Subscribers receive a table of contents; deposited materials must be specifically requested from a listserver. Enquiries may be sent to Lee at the CTI Centre for Textual Studies, Oxford University Computing Services, 13 Banbury Road, Oxford OX2 6NN, England; personal e-mail: *STUART @VAX.OX.AC.UK* or *PEB@MAIL.RL. AC.UK*; system mail *HUMBUL@VAX.OX.AC.UK*.

SCHOLAR

Joseph Raben, the founding editor (1966) of *Computers and the Humanities,* has started a moderated conference on Bitnet called *SCHOLAR*. It disseminates news about worldwide activities in language processing, including literary, linguistic and editorial applications. It may provide annotated tables of contents for such hardcopy journals as *CHum* and *Machine Translation* as well as listing of databases and reviews of software, books, and CD-ROMS. *SCHOLAR* has been funded for two years by the Mellon Foundation. Further information is available from Professor Raben (e-mail: *JQRQC @CUNYVM.BITNET*).

Society for Music Theory E-mail Conference and Online Database

The SMT E-mail Conference is a network for the exchange of ideas among members of the Society for Music Theory and others interested in music-theoretical issues. One may subscribe to the conference by sending a message to its administrator, Lee Rothfarb (e-mail: *smt-editor@husc.harvard.edu* or *smt-editor @husc.bitnet*). You will receive a guide to the conference, a list of current subscribers and their e-mail addresses, and a few other informational documents.

The conference has now expanded to include two new services: posting of tables of contents of music-theoretical and related journals and a bibliographic database that may be searched by means of e-mail. The database contains citations to articles and reviews published in the main music theory journals (including back issues). Currently, the database contains citations only, without keywords, so that searches are carried out only on authors' names and on words in article and review titles. As of May 1992 the database contained citations to articles and reviews in *In Theory Only, Indiana Theory Review, Integral, Journal of Music Theory, Music Analysis, Music Perception, Music Theory Spectrum, 19th-Century Music, Perspectives of New Music, Theoria,* and *Theory and Practice.* Search results are mailed back to the requestor, sorted alphabetically, in standard hanging-indent format. New subscribers will automatically receive an informational document explaining how to search the database.

Further information may be obtained from Lee A. Rothfarb, Department of Music, Harvard University, Cambridge, MA 02138; e-mail: *rothfarb@husc. harvard.edu* or *rothfarb@husc.bitnet*.

Facilities

Center for Electronic Texts

The Center for Electronic Texts in the Humanities was established in October 1991 by Rutgers and Princeton Universities with external support from the Mellon Foundation and the National Endowment for the Humanities. It is intended to become a national resource for those in the U.S. who are involved in the creation, dissemination, and use of elec-tronic texts in the humanities. It will also serve as a national node on an international network of centers actively involved in similar activities abroad.

The Center has evolved from an international inventory of machine-readable texts begun at Rutgers University in 1983 and is held on RLIN, the Research Libraries Information Network.

The acquisition and dissemination of text files to the scholarly community will emphasize "good quality" texts which can be made available over the Internet with suitable retrieval software and appropriate copyright permissions. The Center also serves as a clearinghouse for information concerning electronic texts.

Subscription information and access commands for CETH's electronic discussion group are given in the article "Using Networks." Further information about CETH is available from Annelies Hoogscarspel, Center for Electronic Texts in the Humanities, 169 College Avenue, New Brunswick, NJ 08903; tel. (908) 932-1384; fax (908) 932-1386.

Japanese Music and Computer Society (JMACS)

The Japanese Music and Computer Society was established in May 1985. It currently has 240 members. A bimonthly bulletin is published in Japanese. The editors are especially grateful to Keiji Hirata for providing the following English translations of titles of all presentations given in 1991-92.

Owing to space limitations, it was necessary for the editors to select those items that seemed most relevant to the interests of *CM*'s readers.

The program for the Summer Symposium (SS'92) to be held from Sept. 1 to 3, 1992, at Waseda University, Tokyo, will appear in the 1993 issue of *Computing in Musicology*. The program chair for this event was Tomoyasu Taguti, Faculty of Science, Konan University, 8-9-1, Okamoto, Higashinada-ku, Kobe 658, Japan.

Titles of Presentations Given in 1991-92

34th Meeting (Oct. 26, 1991)

Mikihiko Nagasaki (Seisen Women's Junior College):
"The Possibilities and Problems of Automatic Music Performance Using Sequencer Control"

Takeshi Chiba (Fuji Xerox):
"Musical Sound Analysis using Cepstral Representation"

35th Meeting (Dec. 8, 1991)

Tsutomu Harada, Hideyuki Morita, Shuji Hashimoto, and **Sadamu Ohteru** (Waseda Univ.):
"A Conductor-Tracking Computer Music System"

Naotoshi Osaka (NTT):
"OtKINSHI"

Seiji Murai, Tsukasa Tokiwano, and **Takahiro Urano** (Cameo Interactive):
"Introduction to CAMEO INTERACTIVE"

Masaaki Oka (Kawai):
"The Musical CAI System MUSIC DRILL"

Yukiko Tsubonou (Tokyo Univ. of the Arts), **Tetsuya Hashimoto,** and **Takumi Makinouchi** (Misuzu Eri):
"Oekakikun—Let's Draw Sound"

36th Meeting
(Feb. 11, 1992)

Kunio Kashino and **Hidehiko Tanaka** (Univ. of Tokyo):
"The Configuration of Sound Source Separation/Identification System based on Characteristics of Human Audition"

Keiji Hirata (ICOT) and **Tatsuya Aoyagi** (Univ. of Electro-Communication):
"Towards Inductive Learning of Jazz Harmony Theory"

37th Meeting
(May 9, 1992)

Tsutomu Kanamori, Hiroshi Hirai, Kiyoshi Tsutsumi, Yoshihiro Yuba, and **Yasuhisa Niimi** (Kyoto Inst. of Technology):
"Interpretation of Musicality with Chord Progression in Improvisation"

Mitsuhiko Mori (Hamamatsu Polytechnic College):
"Construction of a Computer System for Music with the Application of Network Technology"

Keizyu Anada, Makoto Itami, and **Kohji Itoh** (Science Univ. of Tokyo):
"A Computer Assistant for Composition in Music Education"

38th Meeting
(June 14, 1992)

Kin-ya Kanno (Matsushita):
"Sound Graphics"

Officers of JMACS

President:
  Seiji Inokuchi
    Department of Control Engineering,
    Osaka University J1-1,
    Machikaneyama-cho, Toyonaka-shi
    Osaka, 560 Japan
    tel. +81 6/844-1151 (ext. 4625)
    e-mail: *inokuchi@inolab.ce.osaka-u.ac.jp*

Chairperson:
  Toshiaki Matsushima
    Department of Information Science/Toho Univ.
    2-2-1 Miyama, Funabashi-shi,
    Chiba-ken, 274 Japan
    tel. +81 474/72-1141
    e-mail: *matusima@tansei.cc.u-tokyo.ac.jp*

Board Members

Organizations

AIMI

The Associazione di Informatica Musicale Italiana has established a study group on computational musicology to foster communication between researchers and to facilitate exchange of ideas. Lelio Camilleri is the coordinator.

ATMI

The Association for Technology in Music Instruction invites new memberships ($20/US and Canada; $30/elsewhere), which provide a bimonthly newsletter, a subscrption to the *Journal of Computer-Based Instruction*, and an annual *Technology Directory*, which includes information on a variety of computer-related products. Listings for the *Directory* may be sent to Barbara Murphy, ATMI Technology Director, 1535 Woodbrook Dr. #137, East Lansing, MI 48823. Membership enquiries should be addressed to Ann K. Blombach, The Ohio State University, School of Music, 1899 College Rd., Columbus, OH 43210-1170; e-mail: *ts0183@ohstmvsa.bitnet*.

ESCOM

The European Society for the Cognitive Sciences of Music plans to initiate a news-letter furthering the aim of translating recent findings from cognitive studies into practical applications in music education. Conferences and other vehicles for communications are foreseen. Further information may be requested from Dr. Frans Evers, The Royal Conservatory, Juliana van Stolberglaan 1, 2595 CA 's-Gravenhage [The Hague], The Netherlands; tel. +31 70/3814251.

IEEE

A Task Force on music applications has recently been formed under the auspices of the computer science divisions of the Institute of Electrical and Electronics Engineers (IEEE). The task force proposes to function in four areas—computer music, desktop publishing of music, standards for music and audio technologies, and computer-assisted musicology. It hopes to function as an interdisciplinary forum involving scientists, musicians, musicologists, and engineers as well as specialists in artificial intelligence, perception, cognitive studies, and other evolving fields. Denis Baggi and Goffredo Haus are the principal organizers. Messages and queries may be sent to *music @imiucca.csi.unimi.it*.

Products—CD

CD+MIDI

Warner New Media (3500 Olive Ave., Burbank, CA 91505) released in June 1992 the first commercial *CD+MIDI* compact disk, which features music from Gershwin's *Rhapsody in Blue*.

ESTC

The *Eighteenth-Century Short Title Catalogue* was published on CD-ROM in March 1992. It is also available via the online databases RLIN in the US and BLAISE in the UK. The current version includes 315,000 entries representing single publications, chiefly books and monographs. Much ephemera in the database (libretti, poetry, commentaries on events that included musical performance, etc.) is of value in music-historical studies. Enquiries may be directed to The College of Humanities and Social Sciences, Sproul Hall, University of California, Riverside, CA 92520-0312, or Humanities and Social Sciences, British Library, Great Russell St., London WC1B 3DG, England.

muse/RILM

muse [MUsic SEarch] is the software that accompanies the *RILM Abstracts of Music Literature* on CD-ROM. *muse* runs on MS DOS machines. The *RILM* database, which contains abstracts of writings on music in several hundred periodical publications (including *CM*), and search software are available by annual license only from National Information Services Corp., Ste. 6, Wyman Towers, 3100 St. Paul St., Baltimore, MD 21218; tel. (301) 243-0797; fax (301) 243-0982. This package and the following one are reviewed by Robert Skinner in *Notes*, 48/3 (March 1992), 945-53.

The Music Index

A revised version of the MS DOS retrieval software that comes with *The Music Index on CD-ROM* has been promised by the publishers, Chadwyck-Healey Inc., 1101 King Street, Ste. 380, Alexandria, VA 22314; tel. (800) 752-0515.

OCLC Music Library

The *OCLC Music Library*, a database of bibliographical records for more than 400,000 sound recordings, has been released on CD by SilverPlatter Information Inc., 100 River Ridge Road, Norwood, MA 02062-5026 (800-343-0064); US fax (617) 769-8763; UK fax +44 081-995-5159.

Products—Software

Gregorian Calendar

If you need to determine what day of the week April 3, 1614, was, a shareware program called *The Gregorian Calendar* may save you a lot of hand computation. The *GC* contains a database of dates from 1583 to 2100 and is able to display calendars for any six consecutive months on a PC. *GC*, which costs $15, can be ordered as Disk #2155 from PC-SIG, 1030-D E. Duane Ave., Sunnyvale, CA 94086; tel. (408) 730-9291; fax (408) 730-2107.

The Music Minder

Performing organizations may be interested to know about a PC shareware program called *The Music Minder*, which keeps track of orders, inventories, and performance information and can be searched by composer, title, and keyword.

The program is available for $20 as Disk #1472 from PC-SIG, 1030-D E. Duane Ave., Sunnyvale, CA 94086; tel. (408) 730-9291; fax (408) 730-2107.

MusicSculptor

MusicSculptor is a realtime algorithmic composition tool for *MIDI* sequencing environments on an MS-DOS platform. It has a library of modules for generating music in several styles. It also has routines for mode (major/minor) transformation, transposition, inversion, and retrogradation as well as pitch and octave filters and other features. It is compatible with the book *Automated Music Composition* by Phil Windsor and is distributed by ProGenitor Software, C.I.R.I.A.S., University of North Texas, PO Box 13886, Denton, TX 76203; tel. (817) 565-3185.

Programs of Study

LabanWriter

Workshops to familiarize users with the software program *LabanWriter* [described in *CM 1991*, pp. 68-9] were conducted at The Ohio State University in June and September 1992. *LabanWriter*, which runs on an Apple Macintosh, facilitates the preparation of dance scores in Labanotation. Information on future workshops and on the product may be requested from Scott Sutherland or Lucy Venable at the Dance Notation Bureau, Ohio State Uni-

versity, 1813 N. High Street, Columbus, OH 43210-1394.

Music Technology

New York University has introduced two new degree programs in music—a B.M. in Music Business/Music Technology and an M.M. in Music Technology. Ken-neth Peacock directs the music technology programs. N.Y.U. has been designated a music software development site for Digidesign's *Sound Tools* and for *Max*, an object-oriented user-programmable *MIDI* software environment developed by Miller Puckette at IRCAM and distributed by Opcode Systems.

Enquiries may be addressed to N.Y.U. Graduate Admissions, 32 Washington Place, New York, NY 10003; tel. (212) 998-5030 and tel. (212) 998-5422.

Publications

Applications in Musicology: A Retrospective

Walter B. Hewlett and Eleanor Selfridge-Field provide a 25-year retrospective on applications in music representation, printing, and analysis in *Computers and the Humanities*, 25/6 (Nov.-Dec. 1991), 381-92. They describe paradigms and their residues from the Sixties to the present day. This article complements retrospective views of computing activities in other disciplines to mark the 25th anniversary of *CHum*, which is published in Holland by Kluwer Academic Publishers.

CD-ROM Librarian

CD-ROM Librarian (ISSN 0893-9934) is a monthly publication now in its seventh year. It is offered by Meckler Corp., 11 Ferry Lane West, Westport, CT 06880; tel. (203) 226-6967; e-mail: *Meckler @jvnc.net*.

Cognition of Speech and Music

Similarities between speech and music, especially from a cognitive and perceptual perspective, are emphasized in *Music, Language, Speech, and Brain*, a collection of essays edited by Johan Sundberg, Lennart Nord, and Rolf Carlson for Stockton Press. Among the six topic areas are those considering language and music, speech and music performance, and voice

and instruments. Enquiries may be addressed to Stockton Press, Houndsmills, Basingstoke RG21 2XS, England [ISBN 0-333-56429-4]; tel. +44 256/29242; fax +44 256/810526.

Humanities Computing Yearbook

The second *Humanities Computing Yearbook*, subtitled "1989-90" but not in circulation until the end of 1991, will interest many readers seeking esoteric information on unusual software for text applications. Word-processing programs, principally for the Macintosh and PC platforms, for a very large number of ancient and modern European and near-Eastern languages are listed, and a great many useful addresses and bibliographical citations are provided. A short section on applications and software related to music printing and music analysis is provided by Lelio Camilleri and Eleanor Selfridge-Field. The *HCY* is published by Oxford University Press.

ICMA Video Review

Roger Dannenberg edits the first issue of the International Computer Music Association's *Video Review*. The 90-minute video features interactive computer music demonstrations from many places and includes Paul McAvunney's *Video-Harp*, Max Mathews's *Radio Drum*, and Stephen Malinowski's *Music Animation*

Machine. Further information is available from the ICMA, 2040 Polk St., Ste. 330, San Francisco, CA 94109.

IDEA

The first *International Directory of Electronic Arts* (1991) is a valuable resource for addresses of and other information about museums, galleries, festivals, and conferences involving interfaces between art, science, and technology. Publication of a second volume was anticipated for 1992. The editor is Annick Bureaud. *IDEA* is available for 210 FF ($32US) from Chaos, 57 rue Falguière, 75015 Paris, France; tel. +33 1/43.20.92.23; fax +33 1/43.20.97.72.

Interactive Melodic Analysis

Barbara Jesser's doctoral dissertation (Essen University, 1988) is now available under the title *Interaktive Melodienanalyses: Methodik und Anwendung computergestützter Analyseverfahren in Musikethnologie und Volksliedforschung: typologische Untersuchung der Balladensammlung des DVA*. Her book is published by the firm of Peter Lang of Berne (1991) as Vol. 12 in the series *Studien zur Volksliedforschung*.

Machine Models of Music

Stephen Schwanauer and David Levit are the co-editors of the book *Machine Models of Music*, scheduled for publication by M.I.T. Press. Schwanauer has recently been involved in the development of *MUSE*, a learning system for tonal composition.

The Macworld Music and Sound Bible

Christopher Yavelow's *Macworld Music and Sound Bible* (ISBN 1-878085-18-5) was published by IDG Books Worldwide (800-762-2974) in the summer of 1992. This applications-oriented handbook includes coverage of *MIDI*, digital audio, composition, notation, film, and education. Each section begins with a foreword by a recognized authority[*e.g.*, Don Byrd wrote the foreword to the notation section.

Fourteen notation programs are examined in detail with sample output. A bimonthly newsletter is available to purchasers of the book. Two companion volumes are scheduled for release late in 1992. These are the *Power User Companion* and the *Quick Reference Guide to the Macworld Music and Sound Bible*.

Music and Cognition

The November 1992 issue of *Minds and Machines*, published in the Netherlands by Kluwer Academic Publishers, is devoted to the subject of "Music and Cognition." Contributors include Jim Kippen, Marc Leman, Catherine Stevens, and Eero Tarasti. The guest editor is Lelio Camilleri.

Music, Mind, and Machine

Peter Desain and Henkjan Honing are the co-authors of *Music, Mind, and Machine: Studies in Computer Music, Music Cognition, and Artificial Intelligence* [ISBN 90-5170-149-7], which is available from Thesis Publishers, PO Box 14791, 1001 LG Amsterdam, The Netherlands; fax +31 20/62-03-395.

Representing Structure in *APL2*

Expressions written in *APL2* can represent both musical syntax and musical semantics. In their article "Toward a Lexicon of Musical APL2 Phrases," Stanley Jordan and Erik S. Friis explore these capabilities in relation to streams of digital sound. They apply the concept of vectors to pitch indicators (*MIDI* note numbers, pitch classes, etc.) and vectors as well as Boolean operators to duration. See the proceedings of *The International Conference on APL, 4-8 August 1991, Stanford University, Palo Alto, CA* (a publication of the Association for Computing Machinery, Special Interest Group on APL; ISBN 0-89791-441-4).

Software for Historians

A Guide to Software for Historians, compiled by Donald Spaeth (ISBN 0-9517514-0 9), provides information on more than 300 software programs for historians, archaeologists, and art historians. The software listings provide brief descriptions of features, technical requirements, and contact addresses. Most products listed are available from suppliers in the United Kingdom. The publication is offered for £8 in the U.K. and £10 overseas. Orders may be sent to the Computers in Teaching Initiative Centre for History, University of Glasgow, 1 University Gardens, Glasgow G12 8QQ, U.K.

Systematic Musicology

Since 1987 the School of Music at the University of Washington has produced a significant number of technical reports in systematic musicology. Current offerings include items on computer modelling, acoustics, perception, and music technology. Further information is available from the School of Music DN-10, University of Washington, Seattle, WA 98195.

Textual Studies

A TACT Exemplar constitutes Volume 1 of a new series called *CCH Working Papers: An Occasional Series for Computer-Assisted Textual Studies*. *TACT* is a microcomputer text retrieval program developed at the University of Toronto; CCH is the Centre for Computing in the Humanities there. Text-concordance programs, facilitation of multi-level analyses of text, and algorithms for pattern recognition in poetry are discussed. Pre-paid orders ($18.50CAN or $16US) may be sent to CCH, Robarts Library, 130 St. George St., Toronto, Ontario M5S 1A5, Canada; tel. (416) 978-4238; fax (416) 978-6519; e-mail: *cch@epas.utoronto.ca*.

Understanding Music

Understanding Music with Artificial Intelligence [ISBN 0-262-52170-9], edited by Otto Laske, is now available from M.I.T. Press. Questions may be directed to the editor by e-mail: *laske@cs.bu.edu*.

Calls for Participation

Archiving Sheet Music

On behalf of a bibliographical project at Duke University, Jeff Perry would like to find a way of indexing sheet music by playing a few bars into a *MIDI* keyboard and then searching a database for the names of all tunes with similar melodic characteristics. Suggestions may be addressed to the Department of Music, Duke University, Durham, NC 27706; tel. (919) 681-6235; e-mail: *JEFF@DUKEVM. BITNET.*

Indian Classical Music

At the Centre for Development of Advanced Computing, Pune, India, Rajeev Upadhye is working on computational aspects of Indian classical music and its automatic composition. He wishes to hear from those working with a similar goal in the context of western music and to find software testers for his research. Messages may be sent to the Centre for Development of Advanced Computing, University Campus, Ganesh Khind, Pune 411 007, India; fax: +91 212/337551; e-mail: *music@parcom. ernet.in.*

Computer Music Software Archive

Roger Dannenberg suggests the organization of information about non-commercial software for computer music. He proposes that there be established a directory of software names and descriptions, an archive of programs, an e-mail archive indexed by topic, and a mailing list to notify interested parties about new listings. Interested volunteers may send mail to Roger Dannenberg, ICMA Research Coordinator, School of Computer Science, Carnegie Mellon University, Pittsburgh, PA 15213; e-mail: *dannenberg@cs.cmu.edu.*

Windows Multimedia Extensions

Philip Donner, an ethnomusicologist, wishes to form a programming group promoting multimedia applications in a Windows environment. Anyone interested may write to him at Mediafrica, Box 1046, 00101 Helsinki, Finland.

Index

A Note to Contributors

Computing in Musicology welcomes information on current and recent computer-aided research, emerging applications, and software development. Contributors should stress the value of their research to musicologists. Contributors of technical and scientific material should seek to emphasize the value of their work in musical studies.

Contributors of historical, theoretical, and analytical applications are encouraged to state how their work is related to other computer-assisted work with similar goals and how their approach could be adapted to other topics. Illustrations that capture the essence of the capability described are highly desirable.

Contributions of more than a few pages should be accompanied by an abstract. Contributions of any length in languages other than English, French, German, or Italian should be accompanied by a résumé in English. It is often helpful to have reference materials in the native language of the author when the submission is in English used as a second language. Much of the material presented in *Computing in Musicology* is condensed. It is therefore to the contributor's advantage to provide succinct information. The editors reserve the right to select those items considered most timely and appropriate.

To be considered for publication within the calendar year, contributions must be received by March 31. Highly specialized materials may be held over for a topical survey at a later date.

All contributions should be addressed to *Computing in Musicology*, Center for Computer Assisted Research in the Humanities, 525 Middlefield Road, Suite 120, Menlo Park, CA 94025. Short contributions without illustrations may be sent by electronic mail (provided that they are **not** formatted for a particular program or printer); these should be identified clearly as contributions to *Computing in Musicology* and must be accompanied by a complete name, mailing address, and telephone number.

Contributions containing bibliographical citations should be provided when possible both in writing and on a 3.5" or 5.25" diskette readable on an MS DOS machine. Machine-readable submissions should be in generic ASCII or *WordPerfect 5.0* or *5.1*. Only contributions including specially prepared materials (manuals, illustrations, etc.) can be acknowledged.

We thank you for your patience and cooperation.

Computing in Musicology: Style Sheet

Italics: In hardcopy submissions, the following should be italicized: titles of books, journals, and proceedings; titles of major texted musical works, such as operas; and titles of programs and specific versions of computer languages (*e.g.*, *Turbo Pascal*) but not of languages (Pascal) or operating systems (UNIX).

Titles: Titles of articles within books or journals, of short texted musical works, such as songs, and of nicknames for musical works (*e.g.*, "Moonlight" Sonata) should be placed within double quotation marks. For titles in English, the main words should begin with a capital letter. Titles in other languages follow native style.

Names: In bibliographical references, please include first names of authors and editors as well as volume/issue numbers (in Arabic numerals) and page numbers of articles in journals and collected writings. Please observe the name order indicated below.

(1) Single author, book:
Mazzola, Guerino. *Geometrie der Töne.* Basel: Birkhäuser, 1990.

(2) Single author, article in journal:
Bel, Bernard. "Time in Musical Structures," *Interface,* 19/2-3 (1990), 107-135.

(3) Single author, article in book or proceedings:
Morehen, John. "Byrd's Manuscript Motets: A New Perspective" in *Byrd Studies*, ed. Alan Brown and Richard Turbut (Cambridge: Cambridge University Press, 1991), pp. 51-62.

(4) Single author, thesis or dissertation:
Diener, Glendon R. "Modeling Music Notation: A Three-Dimensional Approach." Ph.D. Thesis, Stanford University, 1991.

(5) Multiple authors, article in journal:
Hill, John Walter, and Tom Ward. "Two Relational Databases for Finding Text Paraphrases in Musicological Research," *Computers and the Humanities*, 23/4 (1989), 105-111.

Bibliographical listings, which should be limited to eight items, should be given in alphabetical order of the authors' surnames. Multiple references by the same author should be given alphabetically by title.

Citations within the main text may give the author and the year only, *e.g.* "(Hill 1989)". If multiple writings by the same author occur in the same year, please append designations (Hill 1989a, Hill 1989b, etc.) to appropriate bibliographical citations in the reference section.